The Battle for the Republic

Faith, Freedom, and the War for
America's Foundations

Charles Garner

The Battle for the Republic
Faith, Freedom, and the War for America's Foundations

ISBN: 979-8-9924408-6-7

Copyright© 2026 by Charles Garner and PGS Publishing, LLC

Printed in the United States of America. All rights reserved under International Copyright Law. Contents may not be reproduced in whole or in part in any form without the express written consent of the Publisher.

Acknowledgements:

Scripture references are from the English Standard Version, the New American Standard Version (1977), the King James Version. Any others are noted in the text.

Special thanks to the Wednesday Bunch, whose conversations and insights were instrumental in shaping this volume. I am also grateful to the readers who helped hone its message: Greg Adcock, Dr. Daniel Lambert, Rick Latta, Bill Lincoln, Chuck Lyndh, Dr. David Mitchell, Jim Riley, Tracy Sharp, and Dr. Bruce Speer. Their assistance has been invaluable.

Group Study Guide Available

A free, downloadable Group Study Guide is available at **PGSPublishing.com**. The guide provides a structured, discussion-based formation process for use in churches, men's and women's groups, and civic study groups.

In Tribute:

Charlie Kirk

Christian warrior and witness

Author's Note

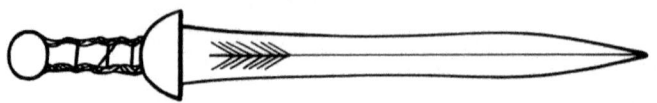

The Battle for the Republic

Nations do not fall in a day. They are weakened over generations—by ideas that corrode their foundations, by elites who betray their stewardship, and by citizens who mistake peace for permanence.

This book is written at such a moment.

The United States did not arrive here by accident. For more than a century, ideological forces hostile to ordered liberty have labored patiently against the Republic—from Marxist theory moving through institutions, to Islamist ambition operating under the cover of tolerance, to the long-term strategic warfare of the Chinese Communist Party. These are not isolated threats. They are coordinated pressures exerted against a civilization that has forgotten how to guard its walls.

At the same time, internal decay has done what foreign enemies alone never could. Corruption, cowardice, and cultural amnesia have hollowed out the nation's immune system. When guardians abandon their posts, invaders need only wait.

This volume tells that story.

The Battle for the Republic is the first of a two-volume companion set. Its purpose is diagnostic. It names the adversaries, traces their methods, and examines how a free people became vulnerable to sustained assault—from without and within. It is not written to inflame, but to clarify; not to traffic in outrage, but to restore discernment. One cannot defend what one refuses to define.

While this volume stands on its own, its full weight is felt when read alongside *Called to Stand*, which turns from the siege to the soul—from the battle for the Republic to the formation of those who must defend it.

If this volume explains **why** the walls were breached, the next addresses **how** they are rebuilt—beginning with the life of the Spirit, disciplined faith, and a renewed church prepared to stand in the public square.

This is not a work of despair. But it is a work of realism.

History is unforgiving toward nations that misread their moment. Scripture is equally clear: discernment precedes deliverance, and responsibility accompanies privilege. In a republic, citizenship itself is a stewardship. Those who understand the times must also know what must be done.

May this volume serve that end.

Charles Garner
Montana, 2025

Editor's Note: Twenty years ago, clarification mattered because access was limited. Today, nearly every reader carries a global library in their pocket. This book is not written to withhold information. Along the way we will mention names, terms, and movements that may be unfamiliar. That is not meant to frustrate you; it is an invitation. When needed, do your own research.

Our task in these pages is to name the patterns and frame the moral stakes, not to turn this into an encyclopedia of dry-as-cracker-dust facts. This is a field manual for warriors. You can often get updated details faster than we could curate them and put them on the page. Some numbers will shift over time—like the fraud case in Minnesota, where totals were still climbing as we wrote—but the patterns remain. Verify what you need to verify. We trust you to do your own work.

Group Study Guide Available

A free, downloadable Group Study Guide is available at **PGSPublishing.com**. The guide provides a structured, discussion-based formation process for use in churches, men's and women's groups, and civic study groups.

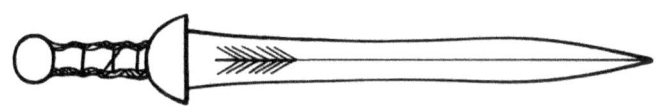

Contents

Prologue *11*

1: *The First Shots Fired* *17*

2: *The Long March* *33*

3: *The Exchange of Glory* *49*

4: *The Creed of Liberty* *63*

5: *The Creed of Equity* *71*

6: *Islamism: The Enemy Within* *93*

7: *The Spread: From Seed to Tree* *111*

8: *The Deadly Embrace* *135*

9: *The Silent Siege* *155*

10: *Parasitic Patterns* *165*

11: *Color Revolution* *179*

12: *Why We Are Weak* *187*

13: *The Great Unraveling* *197*

14: *The Men of Issachar* *207*

Epilogue *213*

"The assassination of truth always precedes the assassination of people."

Prologue

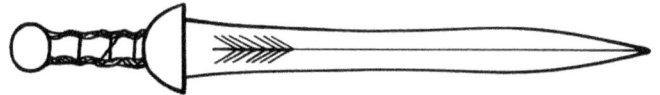

When the Trumpet Sounds

History turns on moments that rouse sleeping giants.

On December 7, 1941, the morning calm over Pearl Harbor was shattered by the roar of engines and the flash of bombs. In hours, the illusion of distance was gone. Long before the bombs fell on Pearl Harbor, Japan had been waging war across Asia — from the occupation of Manchuria in 1931 to the brutal invasion of China beginning in 1937. The world watched, uneasy but distant.

On that December morning, American territory was attacked. The war that had raged overseas had come home.

A stunned America awakened — its slumber broken, its purpose forged in fire. Admiral Isoroku Yamamoto, the architect of the attack, reportedly feared that Japan had "awakened a sleeping giant and filled him with a terrible resolve." Whether the words were spoken exactly that way or not, the sentiment was real — and history proved him right. So it is again.

For nearly a century, a cultural war has smoldered beneath the surface of our nation — a war of ideas, loyalties, and gods. It has marched through classrooms, pulpits, and airwaves, yet many believers have slept through the barrage, assuming the fight would never reach their door.

Then came the shot that could not be ignored.

The killing of Charlie Kirk did not begin the conflict; it revealed it.

It was our generation's Pearl Harbor — a strike that exposed how deep the war for truth has already advanced, how far the enemy has already landed on our own shores.

The sound rolling across America now is battlelines fixed and **shields locking and steel being drawn** — conscience colliding with corruption, faith confronting fury, truth stepping out of the sanctuary and into the field.

The Republic's moral lines are drawn, and the trumpet of God is sounding once more over a church that has grown too accustomed to peace.

This book is a call to arms — not of violence, but vigilance. A call to stand your post, to hold the line, to lift again the shield of faith and the sword of the Spirit. Because the battle has begun, and pretending otherwise will not keep the enemy from your gate.

The Moral Shot Heard Around the World

On September 10, 2025, I was two days into a six-thousand-mile road trip when the news came. Charlie Kirk had been brutally and publicly assassinated.

I was somewhere on the long open miles of the plains with nothing but road and time to think. I'd never met him, though a friend had once handed him a copy of one of my earlier books. That was the only thread between us. But I felt the news like a blow to the chest.

He was thirty-one — young enough to believe history could be shaped, old enough to know it would cost him something. Then, with one shot, that belief and that life ended.

The responses came like artillery over the plains — some sorrowful, some venomous, all immediate. Followers were disbelieving, shattered, yet somehow steady in faith. They grieved and prayed, then sang and prayed again. Others laughed, mocked, and posted their derision in the same breath.

What I witnessed in those first hours was something I had not seen since 1968, when another assassin's bullet cut down a man on a balcony in Memphis.

What was whispered in private then is shouted on the digital wind now. The screen in our hands has become the new front line, where words wound and truth bleeds in real time.

A few days later, a college professor made an offhand remark in my presence that chilled the room: "They're gonna make a saint of him." Not in reverence, but in scorn.

That single comment revealed the condition of the national conscience — the casual cruelty, the studied indifference to loss, the mockery of faith. It was a small sentence that exposed the cracks in our culture's soul.

For decades, we have been told that truth is relative, morality is fluid, and conviction is dangerous. The laughter that followed that professor's words was not spontaneous; it was trained. It was the echo of Antonio Gramsci's prison pen and Marcuse's lecture halls — a century of ideological infiltration that has replaced conscience with cynicism.

The shots you hear now are not just political — they are moral and spiritual. The shot that killed Charlie Kirk was not just a bullet fired in anger; it was the culmination of a long march of ideas that declared war on truth itself.

The Red Line

The blood on the campus in southern Utah marks more than a tragedy. It draws a bright red line through the soul of America.

For decades, while revolutions abroad burned hot and brief, a quieter revolution unfolded here at home. It did not storm the palace; it infiltrated the living room, the classroom, the newsroom, the boardroom, the halls of government — and eventually the pulpit. The long march through the institutions succeeded not because it was fast, but because it was patient. It replaced proclamation with propaganda, truth with "power" language, conviction with ideological obedience.

The long march through the institutions succeeded not with riots or guns — but with curriculum, credentials, and compliant clergy. And while this soft revolution marched, much of the church slept.

We traded the offense of the cross for style and entertainment where technique mattered more than truth. We replaced prophets with performers. Shepherds for showmen. Boldness for branding. Conviction for applause. We forgot that the purpose of light is to pierce darkness, not entertain the already-illumined.

The red line drawn in blood is not merely between left and right, believer and skeptic — it is between courage and cowardice, between the forthtelling of the prophet and fear. It divides a time when the church spoke with conviction from a time when it sought permission to speak.

"If the trumpet sounds an uncertain call, who will prepare for battle?" — 1 Corinthians 14:8

The Call to Inspection

Conflict reveals what comfort hides. Battles do not create weakness — they expose it.

Armor that hangs untouched in a closet gleams nicely — but it does not stop arrows. *Swords* admired instead of sharpened do not cut falsehood. *Faith* unused atrophies. *Doctrine* unproclaimed dulls. *Courage* untested weakens.

This is not the first time America has entered a killing season—just the latest:
1963 — Dallas
1968 — Memphis
1968 — Los Angeles
2024 — Pennsylvania
2025 — Utah

Different years. Same spirit. Same adversary.

We swore we would never walk this road again. Yet here we are.

For decades, pressures have built ideological contempt, spiritual apathy, cultural decay — until the strain could no longer be ignored. These events are not isolated tragedies; they are warnings from the battlefield of the national soul. They tell us that the same forces of hatred, deception, and spiritual rebellion are advancing again.

This book is not a chronicle of despair. It is a field manual for rebuilding souls, churches, and the republic. It will trace how we arrived at this hour, how truth was assassinated in classroom and culture, and how the church can reclaim its prophetic voice.

Endurance is not forged in anger, but in alignment with God's Word, His Spirit, and His unshakable Kingdom.

So test your armor.

Strengthen your ranks.

Wake the watchmen.

Stand in the gate.

The battle has begun, and it will not cease until everything false is exposed and everything true stands firm. And again, the enemy tests whether the church will preach…or hide.

This book is about **discipline and readiness.** It is a manual for building the people of God and ministries that can withstand evil days, stand in truth, and shepherd souls through the fire. It is a rallying cry to pastors and people alike: **take your post.**

Not in anger — but in allegiance.

Not in rhetoric — but in righteousness.

Battle reveals what peacetime hides. Armor that looked polished on the rack either deflects arrows — or fails.

Weapons we admired must now be **wielded**.

Doctrines we affirmed must now be **obeyed**.

Walls we assumed secure must now **withstand fire**.

"Be strong in the Lord and in the strength of His might." — Ephesians 6:10

The hour is late, but the Commander has not changed.

The trumpet is sounding.

Stand up.

Strap on your armor.

Tie your sandals tight.

Lift your shield.

Grip your sword.

Fix your eyes on the Captain of our salvation.

The battlefield is not coming. It is here. Shots have already been fired. Banners are raised. Lines are drawn. Now, as the smoke spreads and the dust settles, we turn to listen for the sound of the trumpet summoning us to battle. And Christ has not called cowards, He has called **soldiers of light**.

"Having done all... stand." — Ephesians 6:13

1

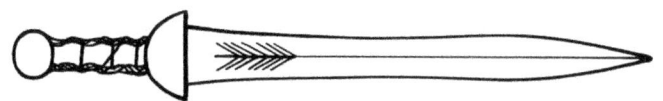

The First Shots Fired
The Battle for Meaning

The sirens had faded, but the echo of Charlie Kirk's assassination refused to die.

Headlines chased theories, and voices filled the air with names and motives. Yet beneath the noise, a deeper silence pressed in — the kind that follows not just tragedy, but recognition. Something larger than a single act had been exposed. The scene of the crime was only the surface; the wound ran through the culture itself.

To ask *who* killed Charlie Kirk is to face one man's darkness.
To ask *how and why* it could happen is to face our own.
To ask *who* pulled the trigger explores a crime;
To ask *how* we reached this moment exposes a civilization.

The investigation that follows will not begin on the campus or in ballistics labs, but in classrooms, pulpits, and dining rooms long forgotten. History rarely turns on a single bullet. It turns on what that bullet reveals. The question isn't merely who pulled the trigger — it's what had already collapsed around the moment that made it possible.

No conspiracy can thrive in a healthy culture; it needs weakness to breathe. And the weakening of institutions — the slow corrosion of faith, family, education, and shared truth — had been underway long before Charlie Kirk fell. Before we can name the culprits, we must understand the conditions. For it wasn't a man, but a culture, that loaded the gun. And the bullet that killed him was loaded a century ago.

The Cultural Battlefield Beneath Our Feet

When a nation forgets its moral code, its words of freedom become stray bullets ricocheting through the public square without aim, intent, or target. Terms that once carried sacred weight — truth, justice, liberty, equality — now rattle like empty shells in the dust. They remain familiar, but they no longer command attention or allegiance.

The blasts shaking our society are not merely political or economic.

They are moral.

They are spiritual.

When truth became negotiable, character became the first casualty. When freedom was severed from virtue, liberty bled in the streets. And when faith retreated to the private sphere, the loudest voices — not the wisest — seized the microphone.

Institutions once trusted as guardians of conscience and civic life — schools, press, courts, even pulpits — now lie under siege. Their ramparts weakened not by sudden assault, but by slow surrender.

America was once a citadel — oceans for moats, industry for walls, faith for foundation.

We did not fall by bombardment.

The gates were not battered down.

We opened them.

Not to armies — but to ideas.
Not to soldiers — but to "experts."
Not to invaders — but to ideologues in cap and gown, carrying textbooks instead of rifles.

Woodrow Wilson unlocked the technocrat gate. The Federal Reserve secured the bankers' drawbridge. The income tax attached the chains and shackles.

By the time Gramsci's thought arrived on our shores, the soil was turned and waiting.

America didn't lose her fortress — she surrendered her foundations.

Not by siege engines — but by deceptive words.
Not by force — but by the counsel of experts.

Troy fell to a gift. Babylon fell to complacency. Constantinople fell to an unguarded gate.
So did we.

A Brutal Killing Awakes a Sleeping Giant

The assassination of Charlie Kirk was not the opening shot of this war. It was the crack of a rifle in a battle long underway — the flash of a muzzle reminding us that ideas do not remain academic. When truth is dethroned, violence becomes doctrine. In such a moment, Isaiah's lament feels written for our hour:

"Justice is turned back, and righteousness stands far away; for truth has stumbled in the public square." — Isaiah 59:14

We are not witnessing the collapse of a nation — but the consequences of a people who ceased to guard its soul.

The Fracture of Meaning

Ideas have consequences. And so does the absence of them.

When Nietzsche announced, "God is dead," he fired a shot not only into philosophy but into the future. The wound traveled through art, literature, education, politics — into the bloodstream of a civilization. For if there is no transcendent truth, there is only power. And if only power remains, every conversation becomes combat; every disagreement, a battlefield.

Truth once served as the shield protecting and binding civilization together. Remove the shield, and the first volley drops even the strongest soldier. We have learned to feel deeply but think shallowly. To demand justice without ever defining it. To applaud passion divorced from principle.

Moral relativism promised liberation — but delivered friendly fire.

Same Words, Different Weapons

Every civilization depends on a shared language — not merely for communication, but for communion. When meaning collapses, unity collapses with it.

That was the lesson of Babel. They spoke one language, and so they marched in unity — until pride lifted their blueprints toward the heavens. God did not topple the tower. He confused their speech, and the people scattered themselves.

We live in a cultural Babel again.

Someone once said to me, "Words don't have meaning; they only have usage." At first it sounded clever. But usage without truth becomes tyranny. If words mean whatever the powerful say they mean, then truth becomes whatever the powerful need it to be.

Consider how language shifts battlefield terrain:
- *Gay* once meant joyful; now it names a sexual identity.

- *Coke* once meant fuel; later a drink; now a narcotic.
- Even *grass* traveled from field to cigarette-papered smokes.

Same words — different dictionaries — different masters.

So it is today with truth, justice, liberty, equality.
> *Truth* is no longer revealed — it is **constructed**.
> *Justice* is no longer righteousness applied — it is **resentment weaponized**.
> *Liberty* once meant freedom to do what is right — now it is **freedom from restraint**.
> *Equality* before the law has given way to **equity enforced by ideology**.

Language has not evolved — it has been captured.

The Tyranny of Redefinition

George Orwell saw this terrain before we marched into it. In *1984*, the state did not burn books — it edited them. It did not outlaw speech — it rationed vocabulary. Control language, and you control thought. Limit thought, and you control the world it imagines.

Saul Alinsky formalized the same doctrine in *Rules for Radicals*: "He who controls the language controls the masses." Call evil good and good evil, and soon the righteous are hunted as rebels. Isaiah warned us: *"Woe to those who call evil good and good evil."* — Isaiah 5:20

Michael Brown put the warning into modern terms: "Control the language, and you control the culture."

When the guardians of language defect, truth waves a white flag. If that sounds academic, it isn't. It's as practical as this:

- When you can't say the truth, you soon stop knowing it.
- And when you stop knowing it, you cannot stand for it.

That's how nations fall — slowly, quietly, one compromise at a time.

Postmodern Babel

Postmodernism replaced revelation's sword with the feather of personal opinion. The target for postmodernism was truth. If the concept of objective truth could be destroyed, then we have no measure for right and wrong. Standards of belief and behavior became the domain of personal choice. In the lingo of the old joke—the Ten Commandments become the Ten Suggestions.

Truth no longer points **upward**, but **inward**. We no longer ask *What is true?* but *What do I feel?* The shift sounds harmless — even compassionate — until one sees its fruit.

Once truth becomes personal preference:
- morality becomes performance
- justice becomes costume jewelry
- repentance becomes optional
- identity becomes a god

The tower falls again — not one of stone but of speech. Not by stones being crushed to rubble but of words losing meaning and definition. Debates rage, yet understanding retreats. We do not converse — we contest. We no longer share meaning — we trade accusations.

A nation that cannot agree on what words mean cannot agree on what reality is — nor what is worth defending, nor what is worth dying for. At that point, the front lines have already been breached. When an appointee to the Supreme Court cannot define what a woman is, we are in trouble. If something so basic to human biology is up for debate, then the walls have been breached and the enemy is in the city.

The Collapse of Discipline

Freedom was never meant to march alone. The Founders tied it to virtue as a sword to its scabbard. John Adams warned: "Our Constitution was made only for a moral and religious people."

The Founders spoke with one voice on this: liberty cannot survive where virtue dies.

- Benjamin Franklin warned that "only a virtuous people are capable of freedom; as nations become corrupt and vicious, they have more need of masters."
- Patrick Henry struck the same chord with even sharper steel: "It is when a people forget God that tyrants forge their chains."

Their message was not philosophical musing but civic prophecy. Freedom detached from virtue cannot stand — it staggers, stumbles, and finally bows. A republic that abandons moral discipline will not be ruled by liberty; it will be ruled by those who promise safety while tightening the chains.

Liberty without discipline becomes anarchy. Indulgence destroys freedom in both the personal and the public life. Like Samson, who refused to discipline his appetites, his freedom and usefulness were lost in the lap of Delilah. A people who cannot govern appetite will be governed by those who exploit appetite. Self-rule dies where self-restraint dies.

Alexis de Tocqueville, peering into the American soul from a foreign vantage point, reached the same conclusion the Founders preached from within. He wrote, "Liberty cannot be established without morality, nor morality without faith."

After traveling the young republic, he saw that America's strength did not spring from her rivers or her laws but from her churches — from a people governed inwardly before they were governed outwardly. The greatness he saw was the fruit of goodness; and he warned by implication that if America ceased to be good, she would cease to be great. Tocqueville stood as the objective witness: ***freedom survives only when it is rooted in faith and disciplined by virtue.***

The Withdrawal from the Field

Faith once stood sentry over the Republic — speaking truth to power and comfort to the broken. Pulpits rang with power. Pews filled with commitment.

But over time, faith was told to retreat: *Private only. Polite only. Harmless only.*

And the church — weary of conflict — obeyed the order. We traded family altars for family centers. We mastered programs but neglected **power.** We filled buildings but not cities with light. We had a form of godliness but denied its power.

Before universities preached unbelief, pulpits stopped preaching the whole counsel of God. When the church withdraws, the enemy does not. The battlefield does not stay empty—it fills with new creeds, promising utopia without holiness, justice without righteousness, salvation without a Savior. Tolerance slid into apathy. Apathy surrendered to silence. And silence, in a moral war, is treason.

The Apostle Paul was dealing with the confusion that had been created in the Corinthian church over the extensive pursuit and use of the spiritual gift of tongues. He used a military analogy to drive home the point that our speech should be clear so the message can be understood.

Paul wrote about the sound of a trumpet in battle. The trumpet was used as a signaling instrument to direct troop movement in battle.

"If the trumpet gives an uncertain sound, who will prepare for battle?" — 1 Corinthians 14:8

When our pulpits censor their sermons, when the church gives an uncertain message—how will either the congregations of followers of Jesus or the needy world know how to respond?

The Hollowing of Belonging

What disintegrated first wasn't the rule of law, but the relationships of belonging.

Institutions once built to bind communities together—churches, schools, the press, even the family table—kept their shape long after they lost their strength. They still stood, but mostly as shells, projecting the image of vitality after the substance had drained away. Like a great tree whose heartwood has rotted, they looked sturdy from the outside, yet one strong wind could bring them down.

By the time the shot was fired on that Utah campus, America had already grown numb to fracture. The assassination only made the fracture audible and evident.

Once, those crumbling conditions were held in check by habits of belonging. Families gathered around tables, breaking bread and sharing stories. Jews kept Sabbath; early Christians shared the Lord's Supper and the love feast; the Navajo, the Amish, the monastic orders — all found rhythm and renewal in shared time and sacred table. Values were discussed, lived, and transmitted parent to child; mentor to disciple; generation to generation.

These were not mere rituals; they were anchors of continuity. They reminded each generation that it was part of something older, wiser, and larger than itself. When the table grew cold, the conversation died, and with it the memory of who we were.

The collapse, then, was not first political but spiritual. When a nation ceases to honor what is holy, it begins to destroy what is human. The Apostle's words written to the Christians in Rome echo across the centuries: *"They exchanged the truth of God for a lie, and worshiped and served created things rather than the Creator."*

Once transcendence is traded for the temporal, the descent is swift. Mind becomes reprobate and the line between freedom and captivity blurs. The gods of progress and pleasure promise light — but they leave only a dark abyss.

The Breach of Institutions

The school once trained minds — now it instructs how to register grievances.

The press once sought truth — now it curates narratives.

Law once defended the weak — now it shields the powerful.

And the pulpit — once the Republic's moral watchtower — too often trades the sword of the Spirit for the applause of men.

Fortresses do not fall overnight but after years of unattended cracks. Destructive ideas breach the walls long before bullets fly. What we now call "crisis" is simply the moment the structure groans under rot that set in long ago.

Yet beneath the noise of collapsing institutions, another sound rises — a deeper, steadier rhythm. Not the drums of revolution, but the marching cadence of a Kingdom that does not retreat.

"The Lord is a warrior; the Lord is His name." — Exodus 15:3.

Listen long enough, and you hear His call through the clamor:
Return to Me. Stand. Be strong in the Lord.

For a nation cannot survive on borrowed courage. If we are to hold the line, we must return to the Commander of truth Himself. The war is upon us — so the trumpet call is to renewal, for us to take our posts, to reclaim conscience, and to stand where others fled.

What is collapsing is not the promise of America, but the pretense of her moral neutrality. Trying to remain neutral is to yield the field of battle. And if we do, the war and the nation are lost. But if we respond, when the false banners fall, the standard of Christ will still be flying.

The Long War for the Soul

Fortresses fall when foundations are neglected, when walls are left unguarded, when sentries lay down their swords thinking the night is safe.

This cultural siege did not begin in our century, nor even in our grandparents' day. It began in European salons and university halls, with theorists who believed that God could be replaced by the State and truth by ideology.

They did not storm the gates — they rewrote the textbooks.

They did not invade the churches — they coaxed pulpits into irrelevance through convenience and fear.

Marxist revolutionary, Rudi Dutschke, named Gramsci's strategy: **"the long march through the institutions."** A revolution not of rifles, but of rhetoric. Not of bullets, but of beliefs.

The clash we feel now — on streets, in schools, in sanctuaries — is not the beginning of that march. It is the moment the enemy reaches the gate. And for those who are aware, the assassination of Charlie Kirk was the attack that roused the sleeping giant, the church of the Living God.

And the trumpet sounds again: *"Watch, stand fast in the*

faith, be brave, be strong." — 1 Corinthians 16:13.

We didn't wake up in this mess as if it had been created overnight. A culture can lose its soul more quietly than it loses a war. The bullet that killed Charlie Kirk wasn't the cause — it was the symptom.

Believers left the wall, ideas filled the breach, and now the smoke of war lingers as the sound of the fatal shot dies. But—the church isn't dead; just drowsy.

In Gethsemane, while the greatest battle in history was being fought in prayer, the disciples slept within earshot of Jesus' anguish. He woke them once, then again — *"Watch and pray"* — but their eyes were heavy, and the hour was dark. They loved Him, but they were not awake.

That scene has replayed across the centuries. Paul heard the same drowsiness settling over the churches of his day and wrote to Ephesus with a trumpet in his pen: don't walk as the nations walk; don't share in the works of darkness; expose them. Walk in love, walk in light, walk in wisdom. Then he sounded the call that rings down our own streets:

> *"Awake, O sleeper,*
> *and arise from the dead,*
> *and Christ will shine on you."*

That is not just a word for first-century Ephesus. It is a summons to the church in our generation — lulled by comfort, distracted by spectacle, tempted to imitate the very world it is called to rescue.

To the Thessalonians, Paul spoke of another trumpet still to come — the blast that will split the skies when Christ returns, when those who *"sleep in Jesus"* and those who are alive and remain will be caught up to meet Him. On that day, no believer will sleep through that trumpet.

But long before that final trumpet, God sounds lesser ones in history — sharp notes of mercy meant to wake spiritual sleepers. Sometimes it's a sermon or a crisis. Sometimes it's the collapse of an institution we thought unshakable.

And sometimes it is the crack of a rifle in the public square.

The shot that killed Charlie Kirk was not the last word. It may yet be a trumpet blast — calling the church to wake, to watch, and to take its place on the battleline again.

Interlude
Sun Tzu in the Modern Battle

The principles that follow were first written twenty-five centuries ago. But they are not relics. They are the strategies our enemies now use.

Marxist revolutionaries, Islamist ideologues, and the Chinese Communist regime have all mastered these dictums. They practice them with precision—deception, psychological warfare, strategic patience, infiltration, propaganda, parallel structures, and the long game of cultural replacement. They know that victory is won long before a shot is fired.

America, by contrast, acts as if no war exists.

The modern Church behaves as if vigilance is a vice and discernment is impolite.

While hostile systems apply Sun Tzu, Western believers drift through an age of existential struggle unaware of the strategies arrayed against them.

These dictums appear here not to teach Christians how to wage carnal warfare, but to expose the tactics already being deployed against our civilization.

You cannot resist what you refuse to recognize.

You cannot stand firm if you never see the ground shifting beneath your feet.

SUN TZU'S 13 PRINCIPLES

1. Know Yourself and Know Your Enemy
If you know the enemy and know yourself, you need not fear the result of a hundred battles. Victory begins with awareness — of strengths, weaknesses, motives, and vulnerabilities.

2. All Warfare Is Based on Deception
Appear weak when you are strong; strong when you are weak.
Confuse, mislead, disguise your intentions.

3. Avoid Prolonged Warfare
Battles drain strength; long wars exhaust nations.
Win swiftly or not at all.

4. The Supreme Art of War Is to Subdue the Enemy Without Fighting
Greatest victories come through positioning, intelligence, alliances, and psychological dominance.

5. Attack the Enemy's Strategy, Not His Strength
Break his plans, disrupt his alliances, undermine his will.
Victory begins long before armies meet.

6. Speed and Surprise Are Essential
Move before the enemy is prepared.
Strike decisively, unexpectedly, and with clarity of purpose.

7. Use Terrain, Momentum, and Timing
Choose the battlefield.
Fight only when conditions are favorable.
Exploit ground, weather, morale, and moment.

8. Avoid Strength; Exploit Weakness
Do not attack fortified positions.
Strike where the enemy is unready, divided, or exposed.

9. Leadership Determines Victory
A commander must be wise, trustworthy, humane, courageous, and disciplined.
The army reflects the general.

10. Discipline, Unity, and Morale Are Weapons
An army whose soldiers share purpose will outfight a larger, disordered force.

11. Secure Supply Lines and Maintain Resources
No army fights without food, weapons, and support.
Logistics often decide outcomes before combat does.

12. Adapt to Changing Circumstances
There are no perpetual advantages; there are only the opportunities of the moment.
Flexibility is survival.

13. Do Not Fight Unless Victory Is Assured
Choose battles selectively.
Engaging in unwinnable conflicts is not courage — it is folly.

This book is a call to recover clarity in an age of deception. These ancient principles remind us that the battle is real, the strategies are ancient, and the danger is growing.

(Dear reader, the next chapter is a long ride across rough country. Long—but necessary. Cinch up, settle in, and keep your eyes open. What you're about to see explains the world you are living in.)

2

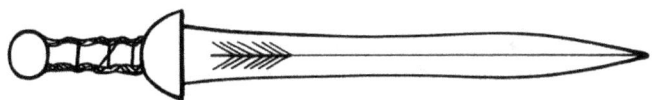

The Long March
The Ideological Invasion of the West

In 1967 the Civitan Club in my small hometown awarded me a scholarship to attend a week-long seminar on the American form of government.

Those were Cold War years—the age of air-raid sirens and "duck-and-cover" drills, when a child's best hope of surviving a nuclear blast was the thin plywood of a school desk. (It must have been remarkable wood; I've often wished I had some of that magic lumber today.)

That week of study opened my eyes. We examined the revolutions that had set the world ablaze—Hitler's fascism in Germany, Mussolini's socialism and fascism in Italy, Lenin's and Stalin's communism in Russia, and Mao's in China. The images still haunt me: gulags, firing squads, starvation, mass graves. Millions were slaughtered and offered on the altars of ideological utopias.

Has the utopian vision of communism ever been realized anywhere it has been tried? Never. *Utopia* literally means "no place" — (οὐ = no; τόπος = place). And that is what has been proven again and again: it is no place...a place that does not exist.

Every attempt to create it has ended the same way—power concentrated in the hands of the few, and ordinary people ground down in the name of a promised future that never came.

Thomas More titled his 1516 work, *Utopia*, as a deliberate pun. The same <u>sound</u> can also mean "good place" in Greek (εὖ + τόπος, different word, same sound). But More's point is clear: the perfect society imagined by men is never found on the map. Five centuries later, history has settled the matter. Every effort to build the "good place" has revealed itself as "no place" at all—a dream that collapses into tyranny.

The most recent failure has been Venezuela. Sitting on one of the largest proven oil reserves in the world, it was once among the wealthiest nations in South America. Life was good — then the socialists promised paradise. Within a generation, shelves emptied, currency collapsed, and hunger became a daily companion. Millions fled to anywhere that would take them. A land rich in oil could no longer feed its own people. That is not an accident; it is the predictable harvest of an ideology that always devours the very lives it claims to save.

Lenin's revolution turned into Stalin's purges. Mao's "Great Leap Forward" became a famine of death. Cambodia's Khmer Rouge emptied its cities and executed its scholars. Each believed that if human nature could be remade, heaven on earth would follow. Instead, they built bureaucratic hells.

The kinetic revolution fired bullets; the cultural revolution fired ideas.

The first sought to seize **territory**; the second sought to seize **meaning**. And in the long run, meaning governs more than armies ever could.

"For though we walk in the flesh, we do not war according to the flesh. For the weapons of our warfare are not carnal but mighty

through God to the pulling down of strongholds."
— 2 Corinthians 10:3–4

The Italian Prisoner and the War for the Mind
In the weeks that followed Charlie Kirk's assassination, I went looking for answers. I wasn't interested in rumor or ideology; I wanted to know how a culture could become complicit in its own undoing. That search led me back through the long corridors of history and, finally, into the writings of an Italian prisoner named **Antonio Gramsci**.

> "The crisis consists precisely in the fact that the old is dying and the new cannot be born."
> *— Prison Notebooks*, 1929–1935

He wrote those words from a prison cell in Fascist Italy, a frail man confined by Mussolini's regime—yet his Marx-inspired ideas would reach farther and last longer than the regime that imprisoned him. Gramsci was not a soldier but a strategist of ideas.

From Kinetic Revolution to Cultural Infiltration
While America watched missile silos and counted warheads, preparing for a kinetic war, another strategist had long been at work—not with weapons, but with ideas. From his prison cell, Gramsci asked the question that would change the modern world: ***Why had Marxism's violent revolution failed in the West?***

Marx envisioned barricades; Lenin executed them.

But in Western nations, the fortresses were not made of stone—they were built on conviction. Family, church, school, civic virtue, moral tradition, and shared identity formed a bulwark no army could breach. Force was useless. Something deeper had to shift.

Gramsci's revelation was patient, not militant: "Socialism will triumph when it captures the culture."

If you could not storm the fortress, you could weaken the foundations. The new campaign would not come with rifles and barricades but through propaganda, entertainment, and education. It would not attack the church; it would imitate it. It would not burn the schools; it would rewrite their creeds.

Gramsci reasoned that revolution in the West required a *war of position*—a slow, generational infiltration of the institutions that shape meaning: "*War of position* ... is the characteristic strategy of modern states, where the front is more cultural than purely military or political."

Before you can change laws, you must change loyalties.
Before you can win the ballot, you must win the classroom.

The battlefield was no longer the palace or the street—it was the lecture hall, the newsroom, the pulpit, and the arts. Gramsci concluded that the West would ultimately be conquered not by bullets, but by beliefs. Revolution would move from the barricades to the bureaucracy, from the shouts in streets to the syllabus.

His insight was both brilliant and devastating: the true foundation of power in the West was *hegemony*—<u>the quiet consent of the governed, secured not through fear but through persuasion, through the shaping of what people call common sense</u>.

"Ideas and opinions are not spontaneously born in each individual brain; they have had a centre (sic) of formation, of dissemination, of persuasion."

Whoever controls what people assume to be normal eventually controls what they believe to be true. The old revolution stormed the palace gates; the new one would rewrite the beliefs people lived from every day. That is where the long march begins.

Paul warns Timothy, *"Guard the good deposit that was entrusted to you."* — 2 Timothy 1:14
Words to live by today.

The Frankfurt School: Seize Minds, Capture the Future

If Antonio Gramsci sketched the blueprint for cultural revolution, the Frankfurt School built scaffolding and framed the building.

In 1923, a wealthy German Marxist named Felix Weil funded the *Institute for Social Research* at the University of Frankfurt. The mission was clear: re-arm Marxism after its battlefield failures. The weapons would no longer be rifles and barricades, but ideas, language, and psychology.

Under the early guidance of Carl Grünberg and later the strategic leadership of Max Horkheimer, a cadre formed: Theodor Adorno, Herbert Marcuse, Erich Fromm, and others in their orbit such as Walter Benjamin. They concluded that *the key to revolution was no longer seizing the means of production, but the means of perception*.

Their tool of choice was **critical theory** — a systematic suspicion aimed at dismantling every pillar of Western civilization. It trained a generation to see all tradition as oppression, all authority as domination, and all moral conviction as camouflage for power. *Critical theory* became Marxism's sniper rifle.

No longer: *Who owns the factory?*
Now: *Who controls the story?*

The battlefront shifted:
- from economics to culture
- from labor to language

- from class struggle to identity struggle

Every institution — family, church, education, law — was reduced to a power structure to be unmasked and overturned. Once that seed of suspicion takes root, no truth is safe; everything noble must be dismantled. From this soil grew the modern worldview that divides society into permanent victims and oppressors — the intellectual ancestor of today's "woke" activism.

Flight — and a New Beachhead
When Hitler seized power in 1933, the Institute fled Germany. By 1934, its scholars were re-entrenched at Columbia University in New York City — carrying not rifles, but notebooks, manuscripts, and the ideological DNA of a new revolution.

They changed continents, but not the mission.

Where Gramsci supplied the strategy, the Frankfurt School supplied the tools:
- Deconstruct belief
- Undermine tradition
- Relativize truth
- Weaponize grievance
- Replace religion with ideology
- Replace citizen with activist

They waged war not on capitalism alone, but on the Judeo-Christian worldview that had shaped the moral architecture of the West. The goal was not simply political change, but spiritual displacement — a new creed to replace the old.

They did not storm churches; their ideas seeped through universities, into seminaries, and finally into the pulpits of America.

They did not burn schools; they rewrote the textbooks.

The March Begins

As their ideas seeped into universities, a new generation absorbed the doctrine. By the 1960s, the theory burst into the streets. German radical Rudi Dutschke called it "the *long march through the institutions*." But the march had already begun decades earlier — lecture hall by lecture hall, syllabus by syllabus.

What began in European seminar rooms found fertile ground in American academia, media, psychology, and eventually theology. The vocabulary of modern identity politics — *privilege, oppression, liberation, deconstruction* — traces its supply lines to those early campaigns.

This was not the revolution Lenin imagined. It was more patient. More subtle. More enduring.

> Marxism traded barricades for bureaucracy.
> Gramsci traded open revolution for quiet infiltration.
> The Frankfurt School traded bombs for books.

And across decades, quietly, almost politely, a new orthodoxy took hold — one that shapes much of our national life today. Cultural capture begins in the institutions that shape belief, not in the institutions that wield force.

- Universities became ideological laboratories
- Seminaries mirrored those academic trends
- Pastors emerged with a softened theological core
- Congregations downstream adopted the softened worldview

***"Beware lest anyone cheat you through philosophy and empty deceit, according to the tradition of men."* — Colossians 2:8**

They understood what many believers forgot:
- Ideas disciple.

- Narratives convert.
- And culture catechizes.
- Before a nation changes its laws, it changes its loves.
- Before it surrenders its freedoms, it surrenders its truth.
- And truth, once surrendered, rarely returns without a fight.

Upstream from Politics

Years later, cultural observer **Andrew Breitbart** captured Gramsci's entire playbook in six words:

"Politics is downstream from culture."

But what, then, is upstream from culture? Montana historian John Fuller answered that in the foreword to one of my earlier books--

> Only by winning the "cultural war" can American Christians win the "political war." The relevant question for Americans concerned about where America is going is, "What is upstream from culture?" The answer is the nuclear family, the church, and the schools. These foundational institutions shape culture, and only by recapturing them can the political battle be won.

The **home, the church, and the classroom.** Those three command centers shape people's worldview. If you seize those, you can steer the nation without firing a shot.

Gramsci's disciples understood that victory begins in the nursery, not the legislature. Capture textbooks and you shape the conscience. Shape the conscience, and you command the nation. The kinetic revolution sought to control **power**; the cultural revolution sought to redefine **good and evil.**

Reshaping what people love, reshapes what they believe—and eventually, what they obey. The *long march through the in-*

stitutions was, at its core, a **march through the human soul**.

"Train up a child in the way he should go" (Proverbs 22:6)**...it works both ways.**

In one turbulent decade and a half, the theory walked into the street.

When the Ground Shifted (1963–1977)

Revolutions don't begin all at once. They start in parallel — in classrooms, in streets, in music, in blood. In the span of fourteen years, America was split down its center. I know, because I was there for it.

In 1967, as mentioned earlier, I sat in a room at Harding College in Searcy, Arkansas, in what they called the Freedom Forum. Harding's National Education Program brought in young Americans and put us through a week of seminars on God, the Constitution, and free enterprise.

We were taught that liberty depended on virtue, that collectivism always ends in control, and that socialism and communism are not just economic theories — they are moral assaults on the dignity of the individual. We were being inoculated, deliberately, against the rise of soft collectivism. They were giving us a spine.

That same year, on the other side of the Atlantic, a German radical named Rudi Dutschke was preaching revolution to students. He told them that the future would not be won by guns in the street, but by a long march through the institutions — schools, media, culture, law. He was putting public language to what Antonio Gramsci had worked out in prison: you don't seize power first; you capture the story first. You capture the storytellers.

So, in 1967, in Arkansas, we were being told to hold the line.
In Germany, they were being told to take the schools.

Two visions for the future of the West, taught in the same moment. And on the West Coast of the United States, a third current broke loose.

That summer, almost 100,000 college-aged kids poured into San Francisco for what was called the Summer of Love that officially kicked off on June 21, 1967—summer solstice. "Turn on, tune in, drop out," they were told. Drop out of restraint. Drop out of inherited morality. Drop out of duty. The language was peace and love; the practice was drugs, sex, and self. People called it liberation. What it really was, was surrender — a moral disarmament in broad daylight.

That didn't happen in a vacuum. Two years earlier, in 1965, Herbert Marcuse — a Frankfurt School philosopher called the "Father of the New Left"— had given the movement its permission structure. In his influential essay, *"Repressive Tolerance,"* he argued that traditional morality, traditional authority, traditional limits were instruments of repression. If the old order was repressive, then breaking it was not sin; it was virtue.

Under that logic, restraint became oppression and indulgence became justice. Thousands of young people swallowed that whole. They walked away from the moral inheritance of their families and called it enlightenment. That generation never fully set that banner down. They carried it with them into business, media, education, government, finance, and — when needed — protest in the streets.

Many of them are still carrying it. And while not everyone who gathered in Haight-Ashbury or Golden Gate Park was a committed revolutionary, in that moment they were carried along by a cultural wave that reshaped the nation.

Then the killing began to crest.

If you want to understand the assassination of truth, look at what followed: the assassination of people.

Assassination

America had already watched a president fall in Dallas in 1963. By 1968, the season of assassination felt like open season. In April of that year, on a balcony in Memphis, Martin Luther King Jr. was shot. Two months later, in June, Robert F. Kennedy was gunned down in a hotel kitchen hallway in Los Angeles.

Two men who, in different ways, could have called the country back from racial fracture and civic despair were cut down within weeks of one another. The message was clear: if persuasion fails, elimination is now an acceptable tool of politics.

When truth is cheapened, life becomes negotiable.

But even that wasn't the end of the upheaval. In 1969, half a million young people gathered on a farm in upstate New York for an event that became myth almost overnight: Woodstock. It was sold as peace, music, and freedom. It was also proof that the counterculture had scaled. The same cohort that had rejected their parents' morality in San Francisco two summers before now anointed its own prophets — the musicians on stage. The soundtrack of rebellion became the catechism of a generation.

And while the crowd in New York swayed and sang, another thread snapped. That same year, 1969, at the University of Michigan in Ann Arbor, a group of self-described student revolutionaries — among them Bill Ayers and Bernardine Dohrn — birthed the Weather Underground. They decided that America itself was the enemy, and they resolved to bomb their way toward its purification.

From 1969 into the 1970s, this group set off explosives, declared war on the United States government, and openly embraced violent confrontation. They believed they were the vanguard.

But here is the part too many people miss, and it matters for our moment: when the bombs failed to produce a mass uprising, the strategy shifted. The war of maneuver — direct attack — gave way to ***the war of position***.

The same people who once romanticized dynamite found their way into faculty offices.

They traded bombs for binders. They stopped trying to burn down the system from the outside and instead walked calmly through the front doors of colleges, teacher-training programs, foundations, media, and nonprofit boards. They entered curriculum. They took up lecterns. They mentored the next generation. They taught education theory, racial theory, legal theory, gender theory, economics, journalism. They carried Gramsci into the classroom and graded the papers.

By the late 1970s, the long march through the institutions wasn't just an idea. It had an address. It had tenure.

Listen carefully: they were far more effective with chalk in their hands than they ever were with explosives.

This is the hinge.

In less than fifteen years, the United States experienced:

- The intellectual justification for throwing off restraint (Marcuse).
- The moral unmooring of a generation (Summer of Love).
- The introduction of a slow cultural takeover strategy (Dutschke channeling Gramsci).
- The public execution of truth-tellers and potential healers (King, Kennedy).
- The weaponization of violence (Weather Underground).
- And finally, the move from street revolution to institutional capture (bombs to binders).

At the very same time, there were people — like those at Harding — still trying to form young Americans in the older creed: that liberty requires virtue, that freedom is not free-floating self-will, that a republic cannot outlive the collapse of its character.

Two gospels were preached to America in that era:
<u>One said</u>: You are accountable to God and ordered liberty is the only soil where human dignity grows.
<u>The other said</u>: You are accountable to no one and liberation is whatever tears down the structure you inherited.

We are now living with the harvest of that split.

This pivotal period — 1963 to 1977 — is not ancient history. It's the root system of our present fracture. The rage in our streets, the corrosion in our schools, the cynicism in our politics, the contempt for faith, the normalization of violence — none of it is an accident. It was formed. It was taught. It was transmitted.

The bullet that killed Charlie Kirk was not an isolated madness. It was the fruit of a doctrine.

And that doctrine did not begin with a gunman. It began with the assassination of truth.

The Quiet Conquest

By mid-century, critical theory had woven itself through the universities of the West like ivy on old stone. From there it crept into journalism, entertainment, and even theology.

Its banner was liberation; its effect was corrosion. Every conviction became suspect. Every truth was called a "construct."

This campaign succeeded not because it was loud but because it was patient. It advanced by degrees—inch by inch, mind by mind. It was like the old mathematical quiz that illustrates the power of compound interest. It goes like this—what had you rather have a $1,000 a day for 31 days or a penny a day that doubled each day for 31 days? The short-sighted view and the error is to take the $1,000 per day for 31 days. It is the patient doubling that really pays off. How much? Try **$10,737,418.23**.

The short-sighted take the $31,000. But patience makes millionaires.

Movements that understand cultural "compound interest" win the long game. Critical theory did not seize. It soaked in slowly, persistently, until the water table of Western thought changed.

By the time the Soviet Union collapsed in 1991, much of its ideological DNA had already been transplanted into the bloodstream of the free world. We had won the **military Cold War** while quietly losing the **war for meaning.**

Out here in the mountains, a fence line will stand for decades if the posts stay solid. But let water seep into the wood and freeze, and the whole thing gives way without a sound.

That's what happened to the cultural West. We were scanning the skies for bombers while saboteurs were already tunneling beneath the walls.

The citadel did not fall by siege—it fell by **neglect**. The long march met no resistance.

That failure ends here! What was stolen through decades of neglect can be reclaimed through decades of faithfulness. We take our post. We hold the line. No retreat. No surrender.

When the enemy threatened to halt the work on the rebuilding of the walls of Jerusalem, Nehemiah gave his men a trowel for one hand and a weapon for the other. We must know that the time of ease is over. We prepare to engage the enemy. And so the question facing believers now is not whether the long march happened, but whether we will answer it.

"Those who built the wall worked with one hand and held a weapon with the other." — Nehemiah 4:17

The Exchange of Glory

The collapse of truth in the classroom soon became the collapse of conscience in the culture. When man replaces revelation with ideology, worship turns inward. And when the creature exalts itself above the Creator, the coup is complete.

What began as an academic skepticism grew into a cultural rebellion, and finally into a spiritual mutiny. The war for meaning became the war for worship.

That **exchange of glory** is the oldest rebellion in history— and its echoes still thunder across the modern battlefield.

"They exchanged the truth of God for a lie, and worshiped and served the creature rather than the Creator." — Romans 1:25

"Tolerance is the virtue of the man who has no convictions."

G.K. Chesterton

3

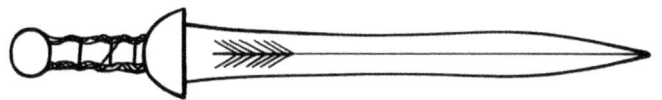

The Exchange of Glory: From God to Man

Recently a man who describes himself as an agnostic said to me, "It seems that the gates of hell have been opened on America."

He's not a preacher. He's not quoting Scripture. But he is describing Romans 1.

Paul wrote:

"And since they did not see fit to acknowledge God, God gave them up to a debased mind to do what ought not to be done.

They were filled with all manner of unrighteousness, evil, covetousness, malice.

They are full of envy, murder, strife, deceit, maliciousness.

They are gossips, slanderers, haters of God, insolent, haughty, boastful, inventors of evil, disobedient to parents, foolish, faithless, heartless, ruthless.

Though they know God's righteous decree that those who practice such things deserve to die, they not only do them but give approval to those who practice them." — Romans 1:28–32

That is not just a private warning about personal sin. That is a public diagnosis of cultural collapse.

Paul lays out a sequence:
1. A people refuse to retain God in their knowledge.
2. God gives them what they demand — life without Him.
3. Their thinking becomes darkened.
4. Their desires become untethered.
5. Their culture begins to justify what it once condemned.

That last step is when it becomes deadly: *"they not only do them but give approval to those who practice them."* Sin is no longer enough for a fallen culture. It must be celebrated. It must be blessed. It must be enforced.

Moral collapse begins not with sin but with applause.

That is what it means to be "given over." That is what it looks like when, in the agnostic's words, "the gates of hell have been opened."

Now here is where the shaking gets close to home.

You and I are living in a country where the two competing moral visions can be summed up in two segments of the same book of the Bible:

- One vision looks exactly like Romans 1:18–32 — unrestrained desire, pride rebranded as identity, moral rebellion not only practiced but blessed.
- The other vision looks like Romans 12–15 — sober-mindedness, sacrificial love, honoring what is good, self-control, service, mutual accountability, blessing those who persecute you, overcoming evil with good.

Those are not simply "religious differences."
Those are two social orders.
Those are two kinds of humanity.
Those are two futures.

The Exchange of Glory

Paul describes the root of all this with one devastating phrase: ***the exchange of glory.***

"They exchanged the glory of the immortal God for images..." — Romans 1:23

Everything else is symptoms. This is the disease.

Human beings do not stop worshiping. We cannot. Worship is not a religious hobby; it is the engine of the human soul. We were created to behold glory — and to reflect the God who gave it. So the question is never "Will we worship?" It is always "What will we worship?"

If a people refuse to worship the living God, they will not become secular; they will become idolatrous.

In the ancient world, the idols were carved in wood and gold. In our world, the idols are carved in ideas. The modern creed sounds sophisticated, but it is the old rebellion in new vocabulary:

- I define myself.
- My desire is my identity.
- My feelings are my truth.
- My autonomy is sacred.

And standing behind that creed is always the same false promise the serpent made in the garden: *"You will be like God."* This is not progress. This is Genesis 3 in designer packaging. The serpent's whisper hasn't changed.

And when a culture baptizes that lie — when it calls rebellion "authenticity," calls holiness "hate," calls restraint "oppression," and calls indulgence "justice" — we are not dealing with bad policy or confused politicians. We are dealing with worship disorder. That is Romans 1.

This is not theory; it is flesh-and-blood reality. And here is the truth the modern church must recover:

A nation does not collapse because it becomes immoral.

A nation collapses because it becomes idolatrous — because it trades the glory of God for the image of man.

Once that exchange is made, a chain reaction begins:
Truth collapses.
Conscience collapses.
Identity collapses.
Law collapses.
Society collapses.

And when Paul says *"God gave them over,"* he does not mean a thunderbolt from heaven. He means something far more terrifying: **God lets a culture have what it wants.**

Billy Graham once called *Psalm 106:15* the most terrifying verse in the Bible: *"He gave them what they asked for, but sent a wasting disease among them."*

C. S. Lewis captured the same truth: *"There are only two kinds of people in the end—those who say to God, 'Thy will be done,' and those to whom God says in the end, 'Thy will be done.'"*

The greatest judgment God can send on a nation is to let it have its own way.

When a people demand life without God, God allows them to taste it — confusion without wisdom, pleasure without peace, power without justice, autonomy without identity, abundance without gratitude. And here is where the church must face its own reckoning.

The God We Forgot—Why soft Christianity cannot save a nation

Soft Christianity wants a soft God — a God of unconditional affirmation but not holy authority, a God who is love but not light, mercy but not justice, comfort but not command. But the God of Scripture is never divided against Himself. His attributes do not compete; they complete one another.

- His love is holy.
- His justice is merciful.
- His holiness is beautiful.
- His wrath is righteous.
- His mercy is mighty.
- His truth is freedom.

This is the God who made nations.
This is the God who judges nations.
This is the God who heals nations.

Unless we recover the whole counsel of God, we will not have a faith strong enough to stand in an age of collapse — nor a spine strong enough to confront the lawlessness erupting around us.

Romans 13 is not an appendix to Christian ethics. It is a divine reminder that justice is a moral necessity, a shield for the innocent, and a restraint for the wicked. And Christians must come to grips with this:

> *A society that refuses to punish evil eventually becomes a society that punishes good.*

We are now living in that inversion. This is why the moment calls not for sentimentality but for courage — courage anchored in the God who is both merciful and majestic, both forgiving and fearsome.

We must do everything faith allows and everything justice demands. Because a nation cannot be rebuilt on a God we have edited. A God we have created in our own image. Idolatry is not just outside the household of faith; it is inside it as well. It is found when we fail to proclaim the whole counsel of God.

Neither the church nor the nation can survive on a gospel we have softened.

Only when we recover the full glory of God — not the God of our preferences, but the God who actually is — will we have the strength to stand against the tidal forces shaping our age.

Into our cultural storm stepped a different kind of voice, standing against the cresting wave that threatens to destroy our nation.

A Different Witness: Kirk and the Students

In the years leading up to his assassination, Charlie Kirk was standing in front of high school and college students resisting the forces of this age. He was saying, in effect:

You are not an accident.

You are not a statistic.

You are not a grievance category.

You are not your urges.

You are made. You are accountable. You are capable. You are called.

That message — not his tone, not his tactics, not his media footprint — that message is what made him dangerous. Because that message is Romans 12-15 in a Romans 1 culture.

Here are the core notes of what he proclaimed to students:

- **Faith / Christian Conviction:** He said faith is not a private hobby. It is the foundation of moral order and the source of human dignity. You are not free because the government says

you're free; you are free because God made you free.
- **Family:** He said the family is not optional or outdated; it is the first classroom of virtue. Strong families produce adults who don't need the State to raise them. One quip put it this way: "Charlie's message on family was simple—Marry, Mate (have children), and Mortgage (buy a home)."
- **Personal Responsibility:** He said freedom and responsibility are inseparable. You cannot be free if you refuse to be accountable for your choices.
- **Moral Order:** He said right and wrong are real, not invented by activists. Truth is not "my truth," it is *the* truth — and it is knowable.
- **Free Speech and Open Debate:** He said if you lose the right to speak, you will soon lose the right to think. Universities that silence dissent are not educating students; they are programming loyalists.
- **Limited Government:** He said the State is not your savior. The State that promises to be your provider will, in time, become your owner.
- **Patriotism:** He said gratitude for the American founding is not bigotry, it is sanity. A nation that forgets the cost of its liberty will lose it.

All of this landed like fire among the young because it spoke to what they already felt but were not being permitted to say out loud.

And this has to be said directly:

Charlie Kirk was not preaching chaos. He was preaching restraint.

He was not preaching self-expression. He was preaching self-control.

He was not preaching revolution. He was preaching return.

That alone should tell you which moral universe he lived in. It also tells you why he was hated. And it explains why he was killed. He had to be silenced.

Recall that a few days after Kirk's death, I was in a small gathering when the college professor of sociology made an offhand remark that chilled the room. "They're gonna make a saint of him," she said — not in reverence, but in scorn.

I felt something shift beneath my feet. The remark wasn't just about one man; it revealed the condition of the nation's soul. The casual cruelty, the studied indifference to loss, the mockery of faith — all of it spoke to a fracture far deeper than politics.

I watched the memorial in Phoenix from afar. Hundreds of thousands gathered — two full arenas inside, thousands more outside in the desert heat. They came not merely to honor a leader, but to testify. Speaker after speaker rose to say what mattered most: that Charlie's hope was not in himself, but in Christ. It was not the event of his death that made him a saint, but the orientation of his life. His martyrdom was not in the bullet, but in the witness he bore.

The professor had been wrong in the most profound way. We did not make Charlie Kirk a saint; his faith in Christ did that long before the shot was fired. His death did not make him a martyr; his life as a witness made him one.

The Greek word for *witness* is *martys*. The exact word we use—martyr: meaning to bear witness, even to the point of death. It affirms something higher than survival. That is what Kierkegaard meant when he wrote, "The tyrant dies and his rule is over; the martyr dies and his rule begins." The tyrant's power ends with his breath; the martyr's begins when his breath is taken.

Kierkegaard went further still — that the "martyrdom of

faith" is not a single act, but a life of continuance. To crucify one's understanding day after day — to live faithfully even when it costs — is the truer form of martyrdom. By that measure, every believer who holds to truth in a lying age joins the fellowship of the martyrs.

History bears this out. The blood of Jesus, Stephen, Jan Hus, Lincoln, Kennedy, and King all fell into the same soil — the earth that receives the righteous when the world cannot. While we do not equate these figures — each lived a different calling — they share this in common: they bore costly witness in a hostile age. And when they were killed, each time, the same strange miracle occurs: what was meant to silence becomes the seed of a new voice.

When a society moves by instinct rather than thought, it lashes out at whatever holds up a mirror. There's a term psychologists use — *mass formation psychosis* — to describe how crowds move as one mind, how panic or ideology can sweep through people until they act without individual conscience or choice.

We see it in nature — birds wheeling in flocks, fish turning in schools — moving as if one body instead of thousands. You can see this same behavior now in nations. It occurs when the herd-mind replaces conscience. And now, this social contagion is carried by the screens we hold in our hands and stare at endlessly.

That, I believe, was at the core of the assassin's madness — an inner war between the values he was raised with and the identity he chose to inhabit. Charlie Kirk's clarity was intolerable to him because it exposed that war. The man could not silence his conscience, so he tried to silence the voice that stirred it. In his world, a social contagion had spread that found its target in Charlie Kirk.

But it never works that way. The bullet that ends a man amplifies his message. The act meant to extinguish truth only throws it into higher relief. The voice he sought to silence was only amplified.

Kierkegaard was right. The tyrant dies and his rule is over. The martyr dies and his rule begins.

The Long March Meets Its Wall

To understand the reaction against him, you have to understand what he was standing against.

Beginning in the early 20th century, Antonio Gramsci, sitting in an Italian prison cell in the 1920s, and later the Frankfurt School thinkers (Horkheimer, Adorno, Marcuse, Fromm, and others) mapped out a patient strategy: if you can capture a nation's culture, you will eventually capture its politics.

They taught that Western civilization itself — family, faith, law, property, tradition — was a system of oppression. And they argued that instead of armed revolution (bullets and barricades), the path forward was slow capture (textbooks and television).

This strategy was later named in plain language by a German radical student leader, **Rudi Dutschke**, in the 1960s. He called it "the long march through the institutions." His point was simple: if you take over the schools, the media, the arts, the legal profession, the bureaucracies, you won't have to fire a shot. The country will already think your way.

That march has been wildly successful.

It began in the elite spaces — Columbia University, the Ivies, the coastal law schools, the Chicago theory circles. Over decades, it flowed outward into state universities, teacher colleges, credential programs, school boards, licensing boards, HR departments. One faculty lounge at a time.

Which brings us to something we have to hold onto:
The sneering professor who said of Kirk, "They're gonna make a saint of him," was not a lifelong radical. She was raised by solid,

conservative, Christian parents. She didn't pick that scorn up at home. She picked it up in graduate school.

That professor is fruit of the long march. She is what Gramsci prayed for and what the Frankfurt School designed — someone who had inherited Christian formation but now holds Christian conviction in contempt, and does so publicly, intellectually, proudly.

That throwaway line — "They're gonna make a saint of him" — wasn't just a personal insult. It was a moral verdict. It meant: "His kind is a threat to the new order."

Of course he was a threat. Charlie Kirk was walking onto campuses and interrupting the pipeline. He was telling students:

- You are not oppressed simply because someone told you that you are.
- You are not righteous simply because you are angry.
- Your feelings are not self-authenticating truth.
- Your neighbor is not your enemy.
- You do not need the State to be your parent.

In other words, he was undoing the catechism of the long march, right in its sanctuaries.

That cannot be overstated. He was not just criticizing policy. He was breaking formation.

Why He Was Hated

We need to say this without flinching: Charlie Kirk was killed because he was effective. He was effective not just at rallying conservative voters, but at interrupting the cultural supply chain — the decades-long, faculty-driven discipling machine that turns 17-year-olds into obedient products of a worldview.

He was young enough to speak their language.

He was bold enough to confront the lies.

He was rooted enough to not fold.

And he was appealing to a moral world that predates the modern left's redefinitions.

He called students back to a framework that sounds, in substance, like Romans 12–15:

- Present your bodies as a living sacrifice.
- Do not be conformed to this world.
- Cling to what is good.
- Outdo one another in showing honor.
- Repay no one evil for evil.
- Overcome evil with good.

That is the life that flows from worshiping the true and living God.

The other frame — the one Romans 1 condemns — celebrates self as sovereign, desire as law, power as virtue, and hostility as righteousness. It blesses rage, applauds transgression, and demands public approval. That frame is also discipling a generation. But its source is not God.

Two moral visions. Two kinds of nation. Two futures.

- One leads to repentance, responsibility, gratitude, order, and hope.
- One leads to pride, grievance, lust, violence, and the demand to be affirmed.
- One vision still bows the knee.
- The other demands the knee.

That is "the exchange of glory." That is why our ground is shaking.

And that is why, if we are honest, what we are watching now is not just a cultural conflict, not just a political conflict, but an act of worship.

When a people trade the worship of God for the worship of man, their laws, schools, and public life inevitably follow. The altar doesn't disappear—it simply changes hands.

In Rome, it moved from the temple to the emperor. In modern times, it moved from the Creator to the collective. Once the Creator is dismissed, morality is no longer grounded in truth but managed by consensus, and consensus soon bows to coercion.

What begins as "liberation" ends as a new form of bondage, wrapped in the language of progress.

The Crossroad

We have arrived at such a crossroad. Two moral universes now contend for the soul of the nation: one anchored in transcendent truth, the other adrift in self-made values. This conflict is not new—it is as old as Eden—but its modern form has become institutionalized, politicized, and global. What we face is not merely a culture war; it is a contest between liberty born of reverence and tyranny born of pride.

From disordered desire to disciplined love—this is the great reversal that distinguishes one moral universe from the other: one, a kingdom of liberty; the other, a kingdom of equity.

"Stand firm, let nothing move you."

— 1 Corinthians 15:58

The Apostle Paul

4

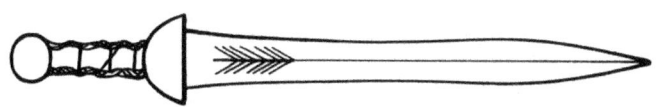

The Creed of Liberty: The First Kingdom

Every age must decide what kind of people it intends to be.

The tremors we traced in the last chapter revealed not only the collapse of meaning, but the rise of rival orders. Before we can understand the kingdom that challenges liberty, we must first remember the one that built it.

This chapter is reconnaissance. We will survey the moral terrain on which the American experiment was founded—its creed, its sentinels, and the enduring architecture that links Philadelphia to Phoenix.

The Battle Lines Drawn

Every battlefield begins with reconnaissance. This chapter and the next are reconnaissance: a side-by-side of two creeds so we can recognize uniforms on sight. What was once hidden beneath the surface now comes into open view.

The tremor that split our age in Chapter 3 has revealed its armies—two moral universes advancing under rival banners. On one side stands the **Creed of Liberty**: faith in God, dignity rooted in creation, freedom tethered to virtue, and government restrained by law. On the other side stands the **Creed of Equity**: faith in humanity, morality defined by consensus, and government enthroned as moral arbiter.

Each claims justice.

Each promises freedom.

But they march beneath **different definitions of man**.

We are in a moment like Joshua who challenged the Israelites, *"Choose you this day whom ye will serve* (Joshua 24:15)." The choice is ours, but the consequences will touch everyone.

The First Formation: The Creed of Liberty—The Founders' Moral World

The American Founders were not moral saints; they were moral realists.

They understood the crooked timber of the human soul and built a system designed to restrain it. Though imperfect men-- flawed, inconsistent, and in some cases hypocritical--they did agree on one bedrock conviction: liberty cannot survive without virtue, and virtue cannot survive without a moral order grounded in something higher than the State. Behind parchment and protest stood that single conviction: **liberty cannot live without virtue, and virtue cannot live without God.**

Here are the core values that shaped their work:
- **Faith in Divine Providence** – A conviction that liberty depends upon moral order rooted in divine law. This is seen in the Declaration of Independence: "endowed by their Creator…" and when President Washington spoke of "religion and morality" as "indispensable supports."
- **Natural Rights and Human Equality** – The belief that all

men are created equal in moral worth and are born with rights that precede government.
- **Virtue and Self-Government** – Freedom is sustainable only when citizens govern themselves morally. John Adams wrote: "Our Constitution was made only for a moral and religious people."
- **Liberty and Limited Government** – Government's purpose is to secure rights, not grant them. Power must be constrained by law and divided to prevent tyranny.
- **Personal Responsibility and Industry** – The citizen's duty to work, provide, and participate. Franklin called industry and thrift the twin engines of prosperity.
- **Private Property and Economic Independence** – Property is the material expression of liberty; a citizen with his own stake in the soil will defend freedom—owners, not renters.
- **Rule of Law and Justice** – No man above the law, every person entitled to due process. Madison called justice "the end of government."
- **Education and Reasoned Debate** – Jefferson's ideal of an informed citizenry; liberty depends upon the free exchange of ideas.
- **Civic Duty and Patriotism** – The health of the republic rests upon participation, honor, and defense of the common good.
- **Public Virtue and Integrity in Office** – Washington's model: character above ambition; service above self. Or, as Fisher Ames, an often forgotten Founder, said: "Liberty has never lasted long in a nation that has lost its virtue."

In plain terms: they believed human beings were created by God, dignified by that creation, corrupted by rebellion, and therefore in need of both freedom and restraint. Freedom alone would become chaos. Restraint alone would become tyranny. The balance between those two — liberty with responsibility — is what they tried to build.

They built a republic on that conviction, trusting that a people who fear God and love virtue can govern themselves.

The Modern Sentinel: Charlie Kirk and the Inheritance of Liberty

Two centuries later, Charlie Kirk spoke that same moral language in a new dialect. He stood as a watchman for a generation untrained in virtue yet hungry for meaning. His creed was no innovation—it was **the echo of Philadelphia heard in Phoenix**.

Charlie Kirk's core values — taken from his public statements, his work through Turning Point USA, and the testimony of those closest to him — form a creed:

- **Faith / Christian Conviction** — Faith was not a hobby. He saw Christianity as a public truth, not a private comfort.
- **Family** — He called the family the first classroom of liberty. Strong homes produce strong citizens.
- **Free Speech / Freedom of Expression** — He believed the university is the battleground for the future, because when speech dies, thought dies.
- **Individual Liberty and Personal Responsibility** — Freedom paired with accountability. Not indulgence, but stewardship.
- **Limited Government / Constitutionalism** — Skepticism of concentrated federal power; insistence that the Constitution still binds our leaders.
- **Free Markets / Economic Freedom** — Hard work, ownership, and enterprise as moral goods.
- **Patriotism and American Exceptionalism** — Gratitude for a nation built on ordered liberty.

- **Traditional Values / Moral Order** — Defense of faith, family, and the created moral structure of human life.
- **Education Reform** — Pushback against ideological capture in schools; restoring civic knowledge and parental authority.
- **Duty, Honesty, Loyalty, Fair Play** — Those around him called this his backbone: say the thing, take the hit, keep the vow.

He stood inside a known tradition. His creed is not an invention but a rearticulation of the Founders' worldview in a new century.

They believed men were **created, corrupted**, and **redeemable**. Freedom without moral discipline breeds chaos; restraint without liberty breeds tyranny. The Republic balanced the two upon the fulcrum of conscience—a constitution framed for a people who still bowed before Heaven.

From parchment to platform, the moral architecture remains unchanged:

faith → conscience → liberty → law.

That is one kingdom's order—the architecture of liberty.

So: from Philadelphia to Phoenix you see the same moral structure:

- Faith under God.
- Dignity rooted in creation.
- Freedom tied to duty.
- Government chained to law.
- Speech protected so that conscience can breathe.

They would echo the Apostle Paul:
"Stand fast therefore in the liberty wherewith Christ hath made us free." — Galatians 5:1

Liberty, rightly understood, is not license but order under God. The Founders saw it; Charlie Kirk echoed it—a freedom bounded by conscience, safeguarded by virtue, and accountable to truth.

Comparison: Founders and Kirk

Founders' Core Value	Kirk's Parallel Value
Faith in Divine Providence	Faith in Christ
Natural Rights & Human Equality	Human Dignity / Image of God
Virtue & Self-Government	Personal Responsibility
Liberty & Limited Government	Limited Government / Individual Liberty
Personal Responsibility & Industry	Work, Initiative, Stewardship
Private Property & Independence	Free Markets / Economic Freedom
Rule of Law & Justice	Constitutionalism / Fairness
Education & Reasoned Debate Civic Duty & Patriotism	Free Speech / Open Inquiry Patriotism & Service
Public Virtue & Integrity	Courage / Honesty / Loyalty

When we look at the continuity of the Founding Fathers to Charlie Kirk, the throughline is readily seen:
- They have the same root. The Founders often spoke in the language of Providence; Kirk speaks in explicit biblical terms.
- They have the same foundation — that worth is given by God, not granted by government.
- The grammar is identical: no freedom without self-control.

- They share a direct inheritance: power must be restrained.
- They operate from the same duty ethic, framed in Christian language.
- Both believe that property and enterprise are expressions of liberty.
- Both held that the law applies to all, rulers included.
- Jefferson's informed citizen becomes Charlie's un-silenced student.
- Gratitude to the republic was seen as a moral obligation.
- Both believed that character as the precondition for liberty.

When we digest this comparison, the continuity becomes unmistakable. The Founders and Charlie Kirk did not live in the same century, but they lived within the same moral world. They spoke different dialects, yet shared the same grammar. Both began with God as the anchor of human worth; both believed that freedom without virtue decays, and virtue without faith withers. Both warned that government becomes a tyrant whenever the people lose their conscience. And both held that liberty survives not through passion or protest, but through character — a citizenry willing to govern itself before it seeks to govern a nation.

The Founders grounded their vision in Providence; Charlie rooted his in the explicit confession of Christ. But the structure remains unchanged:

God gives dignity.
Dignity demands responsibility.
Responsibility makes liberty possible.
Liberty limits government.
And limited government safeguards the people.

This is the First Kingdom — the moral architecture upon which the Republic was raised. It formed farmers and statesmen, soldiers and scholars, and in our day, it shaped a young watchman named Charlie Kirk who called a distracted generation back to its inheritance.

But every creed eventually faces a challenger. As one kingdom taught that freedom flourishes **under** God, another rose insisting that freedom means freedom *from* God. The next chapter turns to that rival confession — the creed that promises justice without holiness, equality without character, and a liberated humanity unshackled from its Maker.

The battle of our age begins here: two kingdoms, two visions of man, and two futures marching toward collision.

5

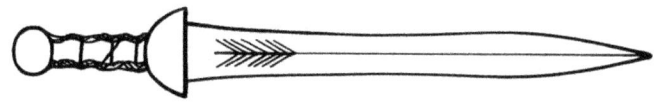

The Creed of Equity: The Counter-Kingdom

While one kingdom was built upon liberty under law, another was rising in the lecture hall. Its prophets carried not rifles but red pens, and its gospel proclaimed deliverance through equality. What began as a critique of tyranny became a theology of man—an inversion of the older order that enthroned self in place of the Creator.

This is that rival creed: the kingdom of equity, born from the long march through institutions and now enthroned in the modern conscience.

The Counter-Kingdom: The New Creed of Man
While the Republic labored to build a fortress of ordered freedom, another empire was assembled in the shadows. Its generals were not soldiers but philosophers—Antonio Gramsci in his cell, and the Frankfurt School in exile. Their Marxist vision enthroned man over God. Marxism is often described as "atheistic communism": God excluded, man installed as the highest authority in the universe.

The purveyors of Marxism such as Gramsci and the Frankfurt School, Rudi Dutschke, and the American domestic terrorists such as Bill Ayers and Bernadine Dohrn concluded (after their kinetic revolution failed) that bullets could not fell the West; only books could. The war would move from battlefields to classrooms.

They taught that truth itself must be **relativized**, faith **ridiculed**, and tradition **re-educated**. The result was **postmodernism**—a campaign not of conquest but of corrosion.

A Rival Creed:
Postmodernism and the New Moral Order

In the last half-century, another system rose quietly to confront that inheritance. It goes by many names — critical theory, cultural Marxism, radical progressivism, postmodernism, "woke" politics — but beneath the labels, the structure is the same.

Here is the core move: it replaces universal truth with lived experience, morality with identity, and God with collective will.

Postmodernism is a reaction against the idea that there is one objective, knowable truth. It claims reality is not discovered but constructed. In this view, "truth" is nothing more than interpretation — and interpretation is always shaped by personal experience, group identity, and power.

In its mature form, postmodernism does three things:
1. It denies universal truth.
2. It treats language and morality as tools of control.
3. It divides society into two categories: oppressed and oppressor.

That last move is crucial. It's the bridge between old Marxism ("workers vs. owners") and what people now call *woke ideology* ("marginalized vs. privileged").

Critical theory — which grew out of the Frankfurt School — trained generations to see every structure (family, church, law, curriculum, biology) as either liberating or oppressive. If an institution preserves any traditional norm, it is presumed guilty. If it resists redefinition, it is declared violent.

This is why the modern Left, at its most radical edge, does not argue with the old moral order — it seeks to delegitimize it. The goal isn't to reform the foundations; it's to replace them.

What began in the Frankfurt classrooms as a critique of capitalism has become a critique of civilization itself — especially the Judeo-Christian framework that gave the West its moral compass.

In the decades since, that classroom vocabulary has become the air of the culture. "My truth" replaced "the truth." Authority moved from revelation to emotion. What began as a graduate seminar now governs HR departments, school boards, streaming platforms, and campaign speeches.

That is not an accident. It is an exchange.

The Doctrine of Postmodernism (in plain terms)

Postmodernism did not arise as a neutral philosophy. It was a rebellion—first against God, then against meaning itself. Where earlier ages sought to discover truth, the postmodern mind insists on constructing it. Reality no longer stands as something given, solid, revealed. It is molded, negotiated, shaped by the will of the tribe or the appetite of the individual.

In this world, truth is not revealed; it is voted on. Morality is not obedience; it is consensus. The commandments are not written on tablets of stone but scribbled in pencil by committees and erased when the cultural winds shift. And the deepest insight of postmodernism is also its most dangerous: Whoever controls the language controls the law. Redefine words, and you can redefine reality. Change the dictionary, and you can change the destiny of a nation.

When Paul wrote that men *"exchanged the truth of God for a lie*" and worshiped the creature rather than the Creator, he described the spiritual DNA of postmodernism long before the word existed. What began as a rejection of God became a rejection of truth, and finally a rejection of reality itself. It is not simply a shift in philosophy—it is a revolt against the very structure of creation:

> Reality is not discovered; it is constructed.
> Truth is not revealed; it is negotiated.
> Morality is not obedience; it is consensus.
> And whoever controls the language controls the law.

"They exchanged the truth of God for a lie, and worshiped and served the creature rather than the Creator." — Romans 1:25

The French Front for Postmodernism

Every revolution has its generals. For the postmodern revolution, the command center was Paris.

- *Michel Foucault* charted the hidden arteries of power, arguing that truth is merely the mask worn by those who wish to rule. He mapped how power operates in institutions where truth becomes a tool of control. In his vision, knowledge exists not to illuminate, but to dominate. What Scripture calls sin, he called "social construction." What the Bible names truth, he labeled an instrument of control.
- *Jacques Derrida* went even further—deconstructing language—making meaning forever unstable. He took a scalpel to language itself, slicing every sentence until no stable meaning remained. If words have no fixed definition, then Scripture has no authority, doctrine has no boundary, and morality has no anchor. Meaning becomes mist—felt, never held.
- *Jean-François Lyotard* gave the revolution its manifesto, de-

claring an "incredulity toward metanarratives"—a formal rejection of any story larger than the self. The grand truths that once bound civilizations together—creation, covenant, redemption, justice—became objects of suspicion. The individual became the only remaining authority.

- And **Jean Baudrillard** foresaw the age when images would seem more real than reality itself.

He sounded the prophecy of our digital age: a world where appearances replace truth, where images eclipse reality, where simulations become more persuasive than Scripture, history, or lived experience. In his imagination, the future would belong to those who mastered illusion—and he was right.

The French thinkers wrote the theory. American universities taught it. Hollywood filmed the sequel. And now an entire generation has been raised inside that story without ever knowing they were characters in someone else's script.

The American Conversion

By the 1970s, these ideas crossed the Atlantic and found converts in media and academia.

What began as philosophical doubt became cultural doctrine: no one owns the truth, and feelings outrank facts. And one of the great proclaimers of this pagan gospel was none other than Oprah Winfrey. Invited into the homes of millions of Americans of all socio-economic strata, regardless of "race, creed or color"—all were indoctrinated painlessly every Monday through Friday. The message sounded compassionate—but it dissolved the conscience.

When all absolutes are abolished, only power remains. The classroom questioned truth; the studio broadcast the doubt; the pulpit, eager to seem kind, adopted the vocabulary of therapy.

Thus the long march turned into a **quiet occupation**.

> *"If the trumpet give an uncertain sound, who shall prepare himself to the battle?"*
> — 1 Corinthians 14:8

The Two Camps

Every political order flows from its moral theology.

Field of Battle	
Creed of Liberty	**Creed of Equity**
Source of Rights	
God-given, inherent	Granted by collective will
Purpose of Government	
Secure liberty	Enforce equality and safety
Moral Authority	
Conscience under transcendent truth	Consensus under shifting norms
Economic Vision	
Stewardship and reward	Redistribution and control
Cultural Emphasis	
Faith, family, tradition	Diversity, inclusion, autonomy

While every institution in America has been weakened or some even captured entirely, the creation of Gramsci and the Frankfurt School found its most comfortable host in the Democrat Party. And to be clear, we are not talking about the Democrat Party of

JFK. That party is gone. Its leaders like JFK have been replaced by politicians who wear the labels of woke, progressives, Democratic Socialists.

These include leaders of the party such as—Bernie Sanders and AOC (Alexandria Ocasio-Cortez)—both Democratic Socialists. And as this text is being written on November 5, 2025—New York City, the seat of the free market in America and influential in financial markets around the world, has just elected Zohran Mamdani, a Muslim and a Democratic Socialist.

More of the party members might identify as "Progressive" Democrats. And it doesn't really matter what they call themselves. In the words of Shakespeare, "A rose by any other name would smell as sweet." What really matters is what they believe. What have they stated as their belief system? When someone tells you who they are, believe them.

The Lineage of a Revolution

Gramsci was not a liberal reformer; he was a committed Marxist revolutionary. So were the men of the Frankfurt School who carried his ideas westward as was Rudi Dutschke who gave those ideas legs in the streets of Europe. When Bill Ayers and cohorts took up the cry in America, they weren't inventing something new; they were translating the same ideology into protests and the halls of education.

The *Long March through the Institutions* was, at its root, a **Marxist strategy**—a plan to reshape a culture from within when open revolution failed. The goal was never simply to critique capitalism, but to re-engineer the moral order that made capitalism possible. The words changed—"critical theory," "liberation," "equity"—but the impulse remained revolutionary.

Over time, the movement shed its red banners and took on academic robes. It learned to speak the language of compassion and inclusion, but the underlying premise endured: that society must be remade by dismantling its inherited truths. That is why today's intellectual class so often mirrors yesterday's revolutionary class.

They may call themselves progressives, democratic socialists, or simply "forward-thinking." Some even wear the label *woke* as a badge of moral awareness. Yet the moral DNA traces back to the same ancestor. From Gramsci's prison notebooks in 1920s Italy to the modern American campus runs an unbroken thread: his conviction that to change the world, one must first change what people believe about truth, goodness, and God.

Gramsci taught that the path to power ran through language, education, and culture—the very terrain on which today's "woke" battles are fought: feminism, critical race theory, DEI, and every group persuaded it is marginalized. In that sense, Gramsci is rightly called the father of modern wokeness.

This is no longer the party of John F. Kennedy's optimism or Truman's patriotism; it is the party of Gramsci's patience—the slow revolution waged not with rifles but with red pens and revised syllabi. The sociology professor who proudly calls herself "woke" may never have read *Das Kapital*, but she is still a child of Gramsci—an avowed communist and revolutionary in ideological lineage. She has absorbed the ideology through decades of education shaped by those who read Gramsci.

Woke thinking sorts the world into two fixed categories — the oppressed and the oppressors. It offers moral clarity without moral complexity, virtue by association, and guilt by birthright. Once that division is accepted, every conversation becomes a tribunal and every disagreement a power struggle.

The grievance industry that has grown up around these concepts takes that same wedge and, with a cultural sledgehammer, drives it into every crack and seam of the republic — race, class, gender, faith, family. What began as a promise to awaken conscience has hardened into a system that keeps people perpetually at war with their neighbors and themselves.

When you call yourself a progressive, woke, or a Democrat, you are a child of Gramsci.

Claimed Values of the Modern Progressive Platform

If you ask what the modern Democrat platform stands for, you'll hear words like:

- **Economic Fairness / Equality** – closing gaps, raising wages, empowering labor.
- **Universal Healthcare / Expanded Access** – care as a right, guaranteed broadly.
- **Education Equity** – equal access, "safe" classrooms, fighting bias.
- **Diversity, Inclusion & Civil Rights** – protection of minority groups and identities.
- **Environmental Protection & Climate Action** – environmental justice, clean energy.
- **Democracy & Voting Rights** – expanding ballot access, opposing "suppression."
- **Immigration Reform & Humane Treatment** – dignity for migrants, pathway to status.
- **Gender & Reproductive Rights / Bodily Autonomy** – abortion rights, gender self-definition, medical access.
- **Faith Communities & Pluralism** – tolerance of many faiths and none.
- **Government Role & Public Safety** – using federal power to ensure material security and reduce harm.

If you listen carefully, you'll notice the moral vocabulary: Fairness, inclusion, autonomy, safety, equity.

You'll also notice what's missing: Sin, personal responsibility, repentance, self-government under God.

Now, to be faithful, we should also name the consistent public criticisms of this platform:

- That "inclusion" often comes with compelled speech and punishment of dissent.
- That "fairness" often means government-directed outcomes, not equal treatment under law.
- That "bodily autonomy" is elevated above the moral claims of unborn life, or created identity.
- That "public safety" and "climate duty" justify expanded regulation and surveillance.
- That the moral law of God is openly displaced by the evolving moral consensus of the State.

You can summarize the difference this way:

Founders/Kirk: freedom first, anchored in virtue, guarded by limited government.

Progressive platform: fairness first, enforced by government, justified by moral narratives of harm and protection.

Both claim justice. But they define justice in two different languages.

Contrasting Creeds: Liberty and Equity

Every political tradition rests on a moral vision of the human person and the purpose of government.

The Founders and those who carry that lineage — people like Charlie Kirk — begin here:

- The human person is a moral agent, created with inherent worth and responsibility.
- Rights are God-given and pre-political.
- Government exists to secure those rights, not to manufacture virtue.
- Freedom is the soil from which justice grows, because free people under God can correct wrongs through conscience, repentance, and reform.

Modern progressive thought, as expressed in the dominant Democratic platform, begins here:
- The human person is primarily a member of a group — racial, sexual, economic, gendered.
- Rights are protected, defined, and effectively granted by the State.
- Government must actively correct inequality, even if it means restricting some in order to raise others.
- Justice requires managed outcomes across groups, which is now called "equity."

We can lay it side by side:

Each side can warn the other of its excesses: liberty without compassion can grow cold; compassion without liberty becomes coercion. But the starting points are different. One believes virtue is the precondition for freedom. The other believes fairness is the justification for control.

And that difference — that split — is not just political. It is theological. The following chart provides an easy side by side comparison of key areas of primary conflict.

Area	
Founders / Kirk	**Modern Progressive Vision**
Source of Rights	
Inherent, God-given, pre-political	Secured and defined by collective action through law
Purpose of Government	
Secure liberty	Promote equality, safety, and managed fairness
Moral Authority	
Conscience under transcendent truth	Democratic consensus, evolving social norms
Economic Vision	
Market freedom, personal stewardship	Regulated markets, redistribution to manage inequality
Cultural Emphasis	
Faith, family, tradition as stabilizing forces	Diversity, inclusion, autonomy as guiding virtues

This is the message and meaning of Romans 1. One side says: "We answer to God, therefore government must bow." The other says: "We answer to one another, therefore government must enforce." One says the image of God is the basis of dignity. The other says identity and experience are the basis of dignity.

That is the exchange of glory.

The Moral Grammar of a Republic

Now we come to a crucial question: do these values reflect, in any way, the attributes of God?

Yes. And that matters.

God's revealed attributes fall roughly into three groupings.

1. Absolute attributes (what God is in Himself):
Immense, eternal, immutable, sufficient, unity.

2. Relative attributes (how God relates to creation):
Omnipotent, omniscient, omnipresent.

3. Moral attributes (how God acts toward us):
Holiness, love, justice, mercy.

When the Founders drafted a republic, and when men like Charlie Kirk called this generation back to first principles, they were — whether they named it or not — attempting to reflect those divine attributes in civic form.

Here's how:

- **Immutable / Objective Truth → Moral Courage.** Truth does not change because God does not change. "Self-evident truths" were not up for renegotiation. Kirk stood in that stream when he insisted that some realities — life, male and female, the created order — are not subject to trend.
- **Unity / Image of God → Human Dignity and Equality Before the Law.** One God, one human race, one shared worth. That is the foundation for "all men are created equal." That is also why Kirk defended the worth of the unborn and the elderly and spoke of borders, citizenship, and national identity in terms of stewardship, not hatred.
- **Holiness → Personal Responsibility / Self-Government.** A

holy God calls a holy people. The Founders said plainly: *if we cannot govern ourselves morally, we will be governed by force.* Kirk said the same to a new generation: *freedom without moral discipline is rot, not liberty.*

- **Justice → Rule of Law.** God's justice is not arbitrary; it is consistent with His nature. The Founders tried to mirror that through constitutional limits and due process. Kirk carried that forward by defending the Constitution as binding, not decorative.
- **Mercy → Religious Liberty and Toleration.** God allows repentance. He offers room for the conscience. The Founders built space for dissent and protected conscience. Kirk did the same when he argued that faith must be free to speak publicly, even if it offends the fashions of the age.
- **Omnipresence / God in all of life → Faith in public, not just private.** We do not carve out a "religious corner" and leave the rest to the State. God lays claim to the whole person, the whole family, the whole nation. That is why both the Founders and Kirk insisted that faith belongs in the public square, not just in private devotion.

So when someone asks, "Is America a Christian nation?" — the honest answer is not "we are righteous." We are not. Are we all Christian? No. The honest answer is *"**our civic framework was consciously built on biblical assumptions about God, man, sin, justice, responsibility, and mercy.**"*

That foundation is what the long march through the institutions has been trying to replace.

From Soft Capture to Coercive Power

Gramsci predicted it: The revolution of the future would not need guns; it would need gatekeepers.

First came cultural hegemony — the shaping of "common sense" through schools, media, and entertainment.

Next came institutional positioning — the placement of ideological allies in key nodes of influence.

Then came policy and enforcement — converting cultural norms into administrative rules.

Finally came the de-legitimization of dissent — where disagreement became "harm" and punishment replaced persuasion.

History shows that once the soft capture is complete, coercion often follows. When ideology captures the conscience of a nation, violence becomes plausible — even righteous — in the service of "liberation." The kinetic and the cultural, the barricade and the bureaucracy, become two sides of the same coin. One storms the gates; the other rewrites the rules.

A Republic Remembered: The Continuity of Conviction
Every generation must decide whether freedom is an inheritance or an illusion.

The Founders declared that liberty was not a gift of kings or parliaments, but a birthright endowed by God. Two and a half centuries later, Charlie Kirk spent his short years calling a new generation back to that exact conviction: Liberty does not survive on slogans; it survives on character.

Washington called it "the indissoluble union between virtue and happiness." Kirk called it "standing for truth in a culture that hates it."

Different words. Same heartbeat.

These men, and every serious disciple of Christ in every age, are answering the same ancient question from Romans 1: Will we worship the Creator, and live within the order He established? Or will we worship ourselves, and demand that reality bow to our desire?

That is the exchange of glory. And that, more than policy or party or platform, is the battleline now drawn across the American republic.

> "The assassination of truth always precedes
> the assassination of people."

The two kingdoms now stand in full view. One rests on the Creator and guards liberty through virtue. The other exalts creation and enforces virtue through power.
Each claims compassion; only one can sustain freedom.

The next movement will ask the inescapable question: *What happens when the church must stand between them?* For the war that began in philosophy now knocks on the sanctuary door.

INTERLUDE — The Blueprint from a Prison Cell

"The most powerful revolution of the 20th century was written by a dying man in a prison cell."

Here's the clear, historically accurate, plain-spoken account of the godfather of the demise of Western civilization and the Marxist capture of its institutions. This is the straight line from **Antonio Gramsci's** Italian cell in 1926 to the present war on the West's foundations—family, school, church.

How Gramsci's *Prison Notebooks* Survived— and Why They Became a Blueprint

1. How the Writings Escaped Mussolini's Prison

When Antonio Gramsci was arrested by Mussolini in 1926, he was expected to die in prison. The prosecutor said openly: "We must stop this brain from functioning for twenty years."

But Gramsci wrote anyway—**3,000+ pages**, from 1929–1935—on culture, education, religion, law, journalism, unions, and the "hegemony" needed to reshape society.

Here's how they got out:

- He wrote in **coded, indirect language** because all notes were monitored.
- Notebooks were kept by Gramsci's sister-in-law, **Tatiana Schucht**, who visited regularly.
- She **smuggled them out page by page** under the guise of personal papers and health reports.

- After Gramsci's death in 1937, Tatiana took them to Moscow, then back to Italy.
- The Italian Communist Party preserved them until after WWII.
- They were published gradually—**no single volume at first**.
- **1948–1951:** The first organized collections appeared (edited heavily for ideological framing).
- **1970s–1990s:** More complete critical editions were released in multiple volumes.

The finalized critical edition is known today simply as *Prison Notebooks*, but it is not one book—it is roughly 30+ notebooks edited into multi-volume scholarly sets.

2. Why Gramsci's Thought Became the Blueprint for Cultural Revolution

Gramsci's brilliance wasn't in class struggle. It was in understanding **why Marxism failed to take hold in the West**. His answer changed the 20th century:

"The bourgeoisie maintains power not by force, but by cultural hegemony."

Meaning:
- Schools
- Churches
- Newspapers
- Family structure
- Civic traditions
- The moral assumptions of a people

...all reinforce a worldview that keeps Marxism from gaining traction.

Gramsci's strategy?
Do not attack the State first. Capture the culture first.

This became known as **the "Long March Through the Institutions."**

It taught radicals that:
- You don't need guns to overthrow a society.
- You need teachers, journalists, seminary professors, artists, bureaucrats, and policy writers.
- You change the meaning of words.
- You soften the moral core.
- You delegitimize the old order.
- You replace its memory.

When the culture shifts, political revolution becomes unnecessary—**the people will vote their own foundations away.**

This was the blueprint that inspired:
- The Frankfurt School (The Frankfurt School was a group of Marxist intellectuals founded in 1923 at the Institute for Social Research in Frankfurt, Germany. Forced out by the rise of Nazism, they relocated to the United States—primarily to Columbia University—where they blended Marxism with psychology, sociology, and cultural theory. Their critical philosophy taught that Western institutions—family, church, schools, media—preserve "oppressive" social order, and therefore must be deconstructed and replaced, becoming the intellectual bridge between Gramsci's cultural strategy and the modern ideological capture of American institutions.)

- 1960s–70s Western Marxist academics
- The sexual revolution
- Critical pedagogy (Freire, Giroux)
- Liberation theology
- Critical race theory (the application of the Frankfurt School's cultural theory to race relations specifically)
- DEI bureaucracies
- Modern activist movements crossing academia, media, and tech

Every single one of those streams draws water from the well Gramsci dug.

3. Why Gramsci Targeted Family, School, and Church

Gramsci argued that these three institutions were the "pillars of bourgeois hegemony":

1. Family

It passes down moral order, responsibility, and identity.

Marxism cannot function where mothers and fathers form independent moral citizens. This weakening and destruction of the family worked its way through the feminist movement, the de-valuing of fathers, the diminished role of motherhood, and millions of other messages that reinforced this destruction.

2. School

It forms thinking, memory, historical narrative, and civic loyalty.

Control the curriculum, control the future. And where did they begin—they began by infiltrating the colleges that produce the teachers. Gradually the mind virus spread. Gradually, steadily, generation by generation.

3. Church

The most powerful of all in his view. Why? Because it teaches:
- objective truth
- moral absolutes
- identity rooted in God, not the State
- allegiance to something higher than political authority

A people anchored to transcendent truth cannot be manipulated.

Gramsci saw Christianity—particularly moral Christianity—as the *primary rival* to Marxist transformation. So he proposed:
- undermine doctrine
- mock traditional morality
- infiltrate seminaries
- shift churches toward social activism
- hollow out biblical authority
- turn pulpits into places of "social consciousness" rather than proclamation

In other words: **Make the church sound like the culture so the culture no longer fears the church.**

4. How His Blueprint Reached the Modern West

Gramsci never saw his plan implemented.
   But others did:
- **The Frankfurt School** refined his ideas in sociology, psychology, and critical theory.
- **1960s radicals** turned his "cultural hegemony" into activism and education policy.
- **Universities** adopted his framework through critical peda-

gogy and postmodern theory.
- **Teachers' colleges** embedded it in training seminars and credential programs.
- **Hollywood and media** shaped narratives reflecting his soft-revolution approach.
- **DEI bureaucracies** became enforcement arms of cultural re-programming.

Today, every major battleground we have identified—school, family, church, national memory—is contested along Gramscian lines.

5. Why This Matters

Because the enemies we diagnose—Marxists, Islamists, Chinese—all exploit the same foundational weakness Gramsci targeted:

A civilization that forgets who it is.

We will see that this forgetting was not an accident. It was a strategy. A slow, patient, parasitic capture of cultural organs.

> Gramsci explained the rot.
> The Frankfurt School taught the method.
> American institutions swallowed the bait.
> And the church, asleep at the wall, never saw the siege begin.

6

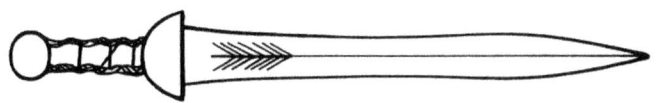

The Roots: From Mecca to the Modern World

How an Ancient Pattern Became a Modern Threat

It was 1979, and the world felt as if it were tilting on its axis.

In Tehran, militants stormed the U.S. Embassy and dragged American diplomats at gunpoint into captivity. The hostages were beaten, blindfolded, paraded before cameras, and held up as symbols of humiliation. Americans sat glued to their televisions every night—first with Walter Cronkite, then with the newly launched *Nightline*—watching the slow bleed of national dignity.

Jimmy Carter, immobilized by caution and a soft, sentimental Christianity, drifted helplessly in the White House. The crisis stretched from days to weeks, from weeks to months, then into a second year. America felt powerless, the West confused, and the Islamic world emboldened.

And right in the middle of that chaos, I moved to Nashville. I was young, newly hired as an editor by the Baptist Sunday School Board—what the world now knows as LifeWay Christian

Resources. The building buzzed with the racket of typewriters, filing cabinets, paste-up boards, and the steady rhythm of an institution still years away from the computer age. Editing was done on paper manuscripts with pencils. Revisions were produced in a typing pool. Memos were handwritten on Post-it notes—the manuscript looked like a porcupine before finished. And everything moved slowly—except one project.

It belonged to Martha Jo Glazner.

She was a veteran design editor—sharp as a tack, quick-witted, and deeply respected. And she was sitting on a resource she was desperate to finish: a study on Islam and Eastern religions meant for churches across America. She worked with urgent intensity, knowing full well that the window was narrow.

One afternoon I leaned on her doorframe while she sifted through a stack of proofs. She looked up and said something I have never forgotten:

"Charles, Islam is the scariest thing I have ever encountered in my long editorial life. It is a violent and aggressive religion. A threat to all of Christendom."

She did not say it in panic. She said it as someone who had looked closely at a system, traced its history, weighed its claims, and recognized its nature.

But the machinery of denominational publishing could not turn quickly enough. Production schedules were slow. Approval meetings took time. Shaping the resource was a laborious process. While Martha Jo raced, the system ambled. And then, before her project could see daylight, the crisis changed.

The hostages were freed.

Not by negotiation. Not by diplomacy. But literally within minutes of Ronald Reagan placing his hand on the Bible and taking the presidential oath.

The moment Carter stepped out, Khomeini stepped back. The hostages boarded planes. The yellow ribbons came down. The nightly television vigil ended. America, with its short attention span and longer desire for comfort, decided the danger had passed.

Martha Jo's project missed its window. The resource was shelved. Churches that might have been awakened remained asleep.

Islamic radicalism, having tested the resolve of the West and found it lacking, continued its long march. At the time, almost no one saw 1979 as the beginning of a pattern. It was treated as a single crisis: dramatic, frightening, painful—but temporary. Once the hostages came home, Americans exhaled and moved on.

History did not.

In the years that followed, the tremors kept coming:

- Beirut.
- TWA 847.
- The first World Trade Center bombing.
- Khobar Towers.
- The embassy bombings in Kenya and Tanzania.
- The USS Cole.
- And finally, the Twin Towers on September 11, 2001.

Each attack was filed under "terrorism," analyzed as a discrete event, and then absorbed into the news cycle. The West treated them as isolated eruptions, products of local anger or rogue cells. But the Islamists did not see them that way.

To them, these were not random outbursts. They were measurements—probing strikes to test Western resolve. Each time the response was soft or confused, the conclusion deepened:

The West will not fight.

The West cannot endure pain.
The West will submit.
The West believed the danger came from "terrorism."

The Islamists believed the danger came from Western weakness. Both believed they were reading reality correctly. Only one was.

And this is where the story of Islamism in America must truly begin—not with 9/11, not with Minneapolis, not with Dearborn, but with the fundamental insight that Martha Jo glimpsed across her cluttered desk in 1979: Islamism is not simply a private religion. It is a political theology with a civilizational mission.

To understand how that mission operates today—in Europe, in North Africa, in the Middle East, and now in the United States—you have to go far beyond Tehran. You have to go back to the seventh century, to two cities separated by a desert and defined by a pivot: **Mecca** and **Medina**.

Understanding that pivot is the key that unlocks the rest of this chapter. This chapter explains the roots of Islamism; the next will show its routes into America.

The Mecca–Medina Framework: Islam's Split Identity

Most Americans think of Islam the way they think of Christianity: as a faith tradition with worship practices, holy texts, and moral teachings that believers can either follow or ignore in the privacy of their own lives. But Islam, from its earliest days, was never merely a set of devotions. It was a total way of life—religious, legal, political, military, and civilizational.

You can see this most clearly in the sharp divide between the two great phases of Muhammad's career. The first phase was Mecca.

For thirteen years, Muhammad lived and preached in Mecca

as a minority voice without political power. His followers were few. His message was resisted by the city's leading clans. The Qur'anic revelations of that period emphasize patience, endurance, prayer, and persuasion. Christians and Jews are addressed respectfully as "People of the Book." These passages—which Western apologists love to quote—sound conciliatory, tolerant, even ecumenical.

But Mecca was the posture of weakness. Muhammad had no army, no territory, and no mechanism to enforce his teaching. In that environment, survival required persuasion, not coercion.

The pivot came in A.D. 622, when Muhammad and his followers fled Mecca under pressure and migrated to Yathrib—later called Medina. That migration, the *Hijra*, marks year one of the Islamic calendar for a reason. It was not simply a change of address. It was a change of role.

In Medina, Muhammad was no longer a persecuted preacher. He became a head of state.
There:

- He formed alliances with local tribes.
- He established legal authority.
- He organized armed raids on the caravans of his former opponents.
- He negotiated treaties—and abrogated them when it suited strategic aims.
- He defeated and expelled or subjugated the Jewish tribes of the city.
- He linked religious loyalty to political obedience.

In Mecca, Islam survived.
In Medina, Islam ruled.

The Qur'anic revelations of the Medina period reflect this transformation. They introduce detailed laws, regulate public life, authorize warfare, and spell out the status of non-Muslims under Islamic authority. Where Mecca speaks the language of patience and coexistence, Medina speaks the language of command and submission.

Classical Islamic jurisprudence recognized this shift and built a doctrine around it called *naskh*—abrogation. When early, gentler verses from Mecca conflict with later, harder verses from Medina, the Medina verses prevail. In practice, this means:

Tolerance is the posture when Islam is weak.

Dominance is the posture when Islam is strong.

That is the Mecca–Medina framework. It is not the difference between "good Islam" and "bad Islam." It is the difference between Islam under constraint and Islam with power. And for fourteen centuries, it has been the operating logic of Islamic expansion.

When Islam is a minority, Mecca dominates the rhetoric: "We want to coexist. We desire peace. We respect your freedoms."

When Islam becomes a majority, Medina emerges in the policies: Islamic law gains privilege. Critics are silenced. Alternative moral visions are pushed to the margins. Non-Muslims are "tolerated" but never treated as equals.

The point is uncomfortable, but it must be stated plainly: Islam adapts its posture to its power.

- When weak, it speaks like Mecca.
- When strong, it behaves like Medina.

You cannot understand modern Islamism without seeing this pattern. You cannot understand the rise of sharia zones in Europe, the political shifts in Turkey, the militancy of Hamas, the intransigence of Iran, or the long game of the Muslim Brotherhood if you ignore Mecca and Medina.

And you cannot understand what is unfolding in states like Michigan, Minnesota, Ohio, and Texas or cities like—Dearborn, Hamtramck, Minneapolis, and yes, Missoula—until you recognize that many of the voices calling for coexistence today are thinking in Mecca terms while dreaming Mecca-to-Medina dreams.

From Desert to Empire: Islam's First Civilizational Arc

Once Muhammad died in 632, the Mecca–Medina pattern did not die with him. It scaled.

Within a single century, Islamic armies burst out of Arabia with astonishing speed. Between A.D. 630 and 750, they conquered: Syria and Palestine; Egypt and North Africa; Persia; Large portions of the Iberian Peninsula; Key coastal regions of the Mediterranean.

These were not empty lands. They were the backbone of the early Christian world. Cities like Alexandria, Carthage, Antioch, and Jerusalem were centers of Christian worship and theology long before Rome or Constantinople dominated the story. The church fathers we quote in our seminaries and Sunday Schools wrote from regions that would soon be under Islamic rule.

Under Islamic conquest, Christian communities were pushed to the margins, forced to pay the *jizya* tax as second-class subjects (*dhimmis*), and gradually diminished over generations through legal pressure, social stigma, and demographic change. The Mecca–Medina logic moved from city to city:

First, a small community of Muslims under Meccan-style constraints.

Then, as numbers and power grew, a Medina-style regime consolidating political and legal control.

Europe itself nearly fell. In 732, Muslim armies pushed deep into what is now France before being turned back at the Battle of Tours by Charles Martel. Had that line broken, the cultural map of Europe—and therefore the story of America—would have been very different.

The pattern did not end there. For a thousand years, from the early conquests to the Siege of Vienna in 1683, Islamic powers pressed into Europe. Constantinople fell in 1453, and the great Byzantine capital became Istanbul. Ottoman armies advanced again and again into Central Europe. Only at Vienna did the tide decisively turn back.

Most Western Christians today know little of this. Our educational systems are embarrassed by the reality of religious conflict. We prefer to tell stories of tolerance and shared values, as if the world has always been a United Nations meeting with better food.

But Islam does not share that embarrassment. It remembers its victories—Constantinople, Jerusalem, Tours narrowly missed, Vienna narrowly lost—as part of a continuous civilizational story. The Mecca–Medina engine is not a theory; it is their historical memory.

After Vienna, Islamic expansion slowed. European power rose. Colonialism and technological superiority pushed much of the Muslim world onto the defensive. But Islam did not disappear. It consolidated. It adjusted. It waited.

Oil and the Rebirth of Ambition

The twentieth century changed the equation almost overnight.

Two forces collided:

1. The discovery of vast oil reserves in the Arabian Peninsula.
2. The modern world's insatiable appetite for that oil.

Tribal societies that had lived in relative poverty for centuries suddenly became fabulously wealthy. Sand kingdoms turned into petro-states. Obscure clerics found themselves with access to billions of dollars.

Oil did not create Islamism. It supercharged it.

Saudi Arabia, in particular, used its oil wealth to export a strict, puritanical form of Islam (Wahhabism) around the globe. Billions of dollars flowed into:

- Mosques and Islamic centers from Africa to Europe to North America
- Madrassas and universities training young men in rigid interpretations of sharia
- Publishing houses and media channels promoting Islamist ideology
- Political movements and militant organizations advancing Islamic causes

The West, desperate to keep oil flowing, rarely objected. We bought their oil. They used our money to export their theology.

Once again, the Mecca–Medina pattern adapted to new conditions. The sword of Medina was now backed by pipelines, tankers, and petrodollars. And the stage was set for a movement that would update Islam's civilizational project for the modern world.

The Muslim Brotherhood: Medina in Modern Dress

If Mecca and Medina explain the spiritual architecture of Islam's expansion, the Muslim Brotherhood explains its modern blueprint.

Founded in Egypt in 1928 by a young schoolteacher named Hassan al-Banna, the Brotherhood emerged from the shadow of two humiliations: the fall of the Ottoman Caliphate in 1924 and the growing Westernization of Muslim societies. Many Muslims felt adrift—politically fragmented, morally compromised, dependent on secular elites and foreign powers.

The Brotherhood's message was simple and electrifying: ***Islam is the solution.***

Not just for personal piety, but for everything: society, politics, economics, law, education, and global order. Islam, they insisted, must rise again—not only in Muslim-majority lands, but eventually everywhere.

From the start, the Brotherhood married ideology to organization with remarkable discipline. They built a movement that could embed itself in everyday life:

- Charities feeding the poor and caring for the sick
- Schools and youth programs providing education and identity
- Mosques and study circles deepening religious commitment
- Political branches agitating for legislative and constitutional change

Compassion became a recruitment tool. Food, medical care, and social support were offered with one underlying message: "See how Islam cares for you. Now give your loyalty to the Islamic project."

Yet beneath this benevolent surface lay a hard edge. The Brotherhood's sermons, tracts, and internal documents made their aim explicit: ***the restoration of an Islamic order grounded in sharia and ultimately global in scope.*** Western secular democracy was not a partner. It was a rival system to be outlasted and, when possible, replaced.

Persecution only sharpened that resolve. When Egyptian authorities cracked down—imprisoning, torturing, and executing Brotherhood leaders—the movement did not die. It radicalized.

Thinkers like Sayyid Qutb argued that the modern world had fallen back into *jahiliyyah*, the pre-Islamic age of ignorance, and that true believers were obligated to struggle—politically when possible, violently when necessary—to re-establish God's rule.

Out of this soil grew not only militant groups like al-Qaeda, Hamas, and later ISIS, but also a more patient, calculated strategy for Western democracies.

The Brotherhood learned to use democratic language while pursuing undemocratic ends.

They spoke of "civil rights" and "religious freedom," but in internal documents they described their mission as a kind of "grand jihad" to "eliminate Western civilization from within." They formed student associations, national organizations, and advocacy groups across Europe and North America. They learned the art of lobbying, public relations, and litigation. They cultivated relationships with media, universities, and political parties.

One branch chose the sword of Medina outright. Another chose the suit, the microphone, and the ballot box. However, the end goal was the same.

This is why drawing a sharp line between "violent Islamists" and "moderate Islamists" is often misleading. The differences are not about destination, but about methods and timing. Al-Qaeda crashes planes. The Brotherhood builds school boards. Hamas fires rockets. Brotherhood front groups file civil-rights lawsuits. One shocks the system; the other seeps into it.

Behind both stands the same conviction: ***Islam is meant to rule.***

Parallel Societies: Islamism's Quiet Strategy

At this point in the story, the pattern shifts from armies and empires to something quieter: neighborhoods, schools, and civic life.

Islamism, particularly in its Brotherhood form, recognized a crucial vulnerability in Western civilization: we assume that everyone who comes to our shores wants the same thing we have—freedom, opportunity, and a chance to join the "melting pot." And in many cases, that assumption is warranted. Millions of immigrants have done exactly that, enriching their new homes while embracing their new loyalties.

But Islamism does not want the melting pot. It wants a parallel pot.

Wherever it can, it builds parallel societies—communities living inside Western nations but governed inwardly by Islamic norms and loyalties. These parallel societies are not simply immigrant neighborhoods. They are alternative social orders:

The mosque becomes the central authority.
Islamic schools and weekend classes shape children in
    Quranic categories.
Family and clan networks enforce internal expectations.
Economic life circulates largely within the community.
Loyalty is directed more toward the *ummah*—the global
    community of Muslims—than toward the host nation.

In the early stages, the parallel society looks like any other ethnic enclave. Language, food, and dress set it apart, but the host culture assumes that time will soften those differences. "Give it a generation," we tell ourselves. "The kids will assimilate. Everyone always does."

That was true when the dominant culture was confident in itself and clear about its expectations. It is not true when the dominant culture has lost its center. Woke has rotted the core.

When cultural confidence collapses, the direction of assimilation reverses. Instead of newcomers adapting to the host civilization, the host civilization bends, bit by bit, to the newcomers. Laws are adjusted. Norms are relaxed. Criticism is silenced. Policies are rewritten to avoid "offense." The majority loses its nerve and, with it, its ability to require loyalty to shared values.

Parallel societies are the proof.

Islamists do not need to conquer a nation to reshape it. They need only to plant enough cohesive enclaves, secure enough political leverage, and wait long enough for the host culture's memory to fade.

That is happening now, visibly, in Europe. It is beginning to happen in North America. Chapter 7 will trace that pattern city by city. For now, it is enough to recognize the logic:

- Mecca rhetoric when numbers are small.
- Medina expectations when cohesive enclaves and political leverage are gained.
- Parallel societies as the bridge between the two.

The West's Failure of Imagination

How did the West miss all of this?

Part of the answer is guilt. Western elites have been taught to be ashamed of their history—of colonialism, slavery, Christian influence, and cultural confidence. Guilt became a lever used to pry loose the moral backbone of the civilization.

Part of the answer is naïveté. Secular thinkers assumed that all religions follow the same arc: as societies modernize, faiths privatize. Religion, they believed, would gradually mellow into vague spirituality and moral sentiment. They assumed Islam would follow the same path as Christianity after the Enlightenment—the safe corner of private conscience. They were wrong.

Secularization has certainly softened Christian conviction in the West. But it has not softened Islamic conviction in the same way. For many Muslims, the West's spiritual emptiness confirms their belief: *Western civilization is decadent and doomed.*

Part of the answer is cowardice. Political, academic, and even religious leaders fear being labeled "Islamophobic" more than they fear being irresponsible. They will not say what is true because they do not want to pay the social cost.

And part of the answer is simple forgetfulness. A civilization that forgets its own story cannot recognize old patterns when they reappear. When you no longer remember Tours or Vienna, Antioch or Carthage, you cannot see Tehran or Kabul clearly.

Into that vacuum step Islamists—and not only Islamists. Marxist revolutionaries, radical progressives, and other ideologues also rush in. Many of them link arms with Islamists under banners like "resistance," "anti-colonialism," and "justice."

In geo-political terms call this is called the _Red-Green Alliance_. This alliance is described as being based on shared anti-Western, anti-American, and anti-imperialist sentiments, despite fundamental ideological differences.

It is a strange alliance: secular Jews marching beside groups that call for a new Holocaust; LGBT activists championing movements that would criminalize them; feminists defending regimes that veil and silence women; progressive pastors embracing coalitions that despise the gospel they claim to preach.

Psychologist Gad Saad calls this **pathological altruism** and even **empathetic suicide**—the emotional compulsion to defend the very forces that will destroy you because empathy has been weaponized against reality.

However you label it, it is another symptom of Western confusion. The civilization that once sent missionaries now sends apologies. The culture that once defended the vulnerable now coddles the ideologies that would enslave them.

Islamists take note. They have learned something that many Westerners have not: The West fears being called intolerant more than it fears losing its freedoms. That fear is a powerful weapon.

Two Very Different Kingdoms

At this point, we must draw a line that our culture has forgotten how to draw—Christianity and Islam are not simply two different paths up the same spiritual mountain. They are built on fundamentally different understandings of God, humanity, and the nature of the kingdom.

The kingdom of God announced by Jesus does not advance by coercion. It does not conquer territory with the sword. It does not impose baptism at the tip of a spear. When Christians have forgotten this and reached for the tools of empire, they have betrayed their own gospel. The New Testament is clear: the weapons of our warfare are not of the flesh. Christ's kingdom is not of this world's systems, even as it penetrates every aspect of life.

Islamism does not share that restraint. Its vision of order is explicitly political. Its law is public. Its ambitions are territorial. Its ideal society is not a pluralistic arena where multiple faiths contend in freedom, but a managed hierarchy in which Islam rules and others submit.

Christians are called to persuade, preach, serve, and suffer. Islamists are taught to rule, legislate, subdue, and, when necessary, fight.

We must never respond to Islamism with hatred. Every Muslim is a person for whom Christ died, and many Muslims are themselves victims of the very ideology that holds them. But love and clarity are not enemies. To pretend that Islamism is just another expression of generic "faith" is not love; it is negligence.

A blind church cannot be a faithful church.

A silent church cannot be a watchman.

The Line in the Sand

We began this chapter in a Nashville office, with an editor who saw something clearly long before most of the American church did. She recognized that Islam was not just another religion in the comparative-religions catalog. She sensed the collision coming between a confident political theology and an increasingly confused Western church.

From Mecca and Medina to the first conquests, from Vienna to the fall of the caliphate, from oil wealth to the Muslim Brotherhood, from Tehran to New York, one truth emerges:

- Islamism is a civilizational project.
- It thinks in centuries.
- It adapts its posture to its power.
- It advances where weakness reigns and recalibrates where strength stands.

The West, by contrast, now thinks in quarters and cycles—quarterly earnings reports, two-year midterms, four-year presidential campaigns, twenty-four-hour news bursts, and twenty-second social-media clips. We drift while they dig in. We apologize while they advance. We forget while they remember.

One sentence should haunt us:

"When the West kneels, Islamists have the perfect angle from which to cut off the head of their enemy."

That is not a metaphor in their worldview. Submission is not a gesture of goodwill. It is an admission of weakness to be exploited.

This chapter has traced the roots: the Mecca–Medina pattern; the early waves of conquest; the thousand-year siege of Europe; the catalytic power of oil; the rise of the Muslim Brotherhood; the strategy of parallel societies; and the West's failure of imagination

Chapter 6 has told us why this conflict keeps resurfacing. Chapter 7 will show us how it is unfolding now—on our soil, in our cities, and in places that still believe they are far from the fault line. The roots determine the fruits. The pattern is in motion.

And the church, at this hour, must decide whether it will stand as a watchman on the wall, as warriors on the battleline—or kneel in the courtyard while the gates swing open.

You cannot negotiate with an ideology that sees you as lawful prey.

The conclusion of Thomas Jefferson after meeting Sidi Haji Abdul Rahman Adja, the ambassador of Tripoli.

A civilization that forgets the convictions its enemies live by will eventually be ruled by them.

7

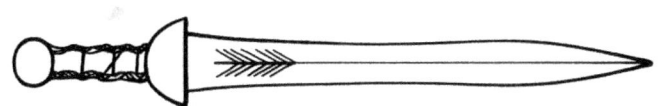

The Spread: From Seed to Tree
Secondary Migration, Demographic Momentum, and the Missoula Signal

Something is shifting in Missoula—quietly, steadily, almost imperceptibly. If you stand in the middle of the city, nothing dramatic announces itself. There are no sirens, no protests, no columns of smoke rising behind the mountains. Yet something is happening beneath the surface, like the subtle groan of timber inside a house just before a winter storm or the faint tremor that warns a rancher the frost has settled deeper than usual.

Most people never notice those early signs. They don't hear the soft crack in the foundation. But you do. Once you know what to listen for, you cannot unhear it. And once you understand the pattern, you quickly realize that Missoula is not experiencing something new.

It is participating in something very old.

What is happening in this Montana valley has happened before—in London, Paris, Amsterdam, Minneapolis, Malmö, and Sydney. It is a pattern with centuries behind it, shaped by a theological trajectory that goes all the way back to the two stages of

Muhammad's ministry: Mecca and Medina. Softness in Phase One; strength and dominance in Phase Two.

Western observers think the story begins today, but the script has been written for centuries.

What look like isolated incidents—an unexpected school-board result in Minnesota, a new mosque in Columbus, a controversial street renaming in Dearborn, a sudden influx of families into a small Idaho town—are not isolated at all. They are linked chapters in a longer story of migration, settlement, and strategic expansion.

Missoula is not an anomaly. It is a signpost. To understand the signpost, we must understand the soil in which it stands.

Part I: Why Islamism Thrives in Soft Ground

Civilizations do not usually collapse because of external invasion alone. More often, they weaken from within—spiritually, culturally, morally. And when a society loses confidence in its own identity, it becomes open to alternative visions that possess the strength and clarity it no longer carries.

The American West is, in many ways, wide-open country—not only topographically but spiritually. The ruggedness remains, but the convictions that once undergirded that ruggedness have thinned. Secularism has not produced moral strength; it has produced moral fatigue. The very institutions that once gave the West its backbone have grown hollow.

Churches that were once filled with families now labor to keep their doors open. Universities that once taught the pursuit of truth now preach a doctrine of relativism so absolute that they hesitate to assert any truth at all. Political leaders avoid moral clarity for fear of offending constituencies that no longer believe in anything fixed or binding.

And into that vacuum steps an ideology that does not waver,

does not apologize, does not negotiate, and does not doubt itself.
Western progressives think in election cycles.
Islamists think in generations.
Legislators look toward 2030.
Islamists strategize toward 2130.
Our agencies evaluate quarterly performance metrics.
Their networks build three-generation family structures, mosque-centered communities, and identity-based cohesion that does not dilute with time.

This gap in generational vision is one of the West's most dangerous blind spots. It is why leaders in Minnesota misread what happened in Minneapolis. It is why observers in Michigan were stunned by Dearborn's transformation. It is why Hamtramck's political shift caught pundits off guard. It is why Missoula will surprise those who believe history only moves in abrupt leaps.

But it rarely does.

History grows like a tree—rooted, slow, patient, relentless. And what appears in Missoula today is not the first branch. It is merely the first visible leaf.

Part II: The Five Phases of Expansion

Americans love the Ellis Island story. Immigrants arrived, built communities, learned the language, adopted the civic order, and contributed to the American story. That was the pattern for much European migration throughout the nineteenth and twentieth centuries.

But Islamist migration, especially in its political and ideological expressions, follows a different trajectory—one shaped by theology, reinforced by modern strategy, and validated by demographic momentum. It unfolds in distinct phases, each building upon the last.

You can see the pattern in city after city, suburb after suburb, region after region. It is not hidden. But it is rarely acknowledged because acknowledging it would require the West to recover its own sense of identity.

Let's walk the pattern slowly and clearly.

Phase One: Gateway Cities — The Soft Landing Zone
Every major Islamist population center in the West begins with a cluster of common conditions. The cities vary, the cultures differ, the languages shift—but the conditions remain strikingly similar.

Gateway cities share several traits:
- A federally funded or NGO-driven refugee or asylum pipeline that brings families in substantial numbers and continues year after year. Often one family member becomes an anchor member. And an immigration train is set in motion.
- A progressive civic government committed to multiculturalism but deeply uncomfortable with demanding assimilation.
- A university environment that champions diversity as an abstract ideal but rarely studies the consequences of parallel cultures.
- A dense nonprofit ecosystem that provides legal aid, social services, translation help, and advocacy—all well-intended, but all operating with the assumption that integration will happen automatically.
- A spiritually soft landscape, where churches hesitate to speak clearly, fearing they might be labeled intolerant.

It is not hostility that creates these gateway environments. It is naïveté.

And once a migration stream begins, the city becomes a "soft landing zone"—a place where newcomers are supported generously but never asked to assimilate meaningfully. Assimilation, in fact, becomes optional. And what is optional is often ignored.

This is how Minneapolis–St. Paul became the first major American hub for Somali migration.

It is how Portland, Seattle, Columbus, and Denver developed their large East African and Middle Eastern enclaves.

It is how San Diego and Northern Virginia became magnet communities for secondary influx.

It is how Dearborn became the symbolic capital of Arab-American political identity.

And it is how Missoula—small, pleasant, progressivist, university-anchored, culturally hesitant—became a landing zone of its own.

The entry point is not the problem. The absence of expectation is. Where no expectation of assimilation exists, assimilation does not occur.

And that moves the pattern to Phase Two.

Phase Two: Enclave Formation — The Quiet Rise of a Parallel Society

Enclaves are not inherently dangerous. Human beings naturally gather around familiarity—shared language, shared food, shared customs. Ethnic enclaves have dotted American history from Little Italy to Little Havana.

But Islamist enclaves differ because they are not merely cultural centers. They become parallel systems—structures that operate beside, and eventually in place of, the local civic culture. Inside these enclaves:

- the mosque becomes the center of community life
- the imam becomes the moral authority

- Sharia norms shape family and social expectations
- halal commerce fills local markets
- Arabic, Somali, Pashto, or Urdu replace English inside the enclave
- clan-based loyalty becomes stronger than civic identity
- communal expectations outweigh individual freedoms

The formation of an enclave does not look threatening to the surrounding city. Early on, it looks like diversity—the kind that earns praise in university brochures. But beneath the surface, the tectonic plates shift.

Schools begin adapting to accommodate the enclave's demands.

Businesses adjust their offerings to attract enclave customers.

Local political candidates court the enclave because bloc voting is efficient.

Neighborhoods shift demographically and culturally.

By the time the city realizes how deeply the enclave has reshaped the local landscape, the changes are largely irreversible. Enclaves, left unintegrated, become alternative civilizational centers. Not violently. Not loudly. But steadily.

And once the enclave stabilizes, it develops enough demographic weight to influence local politics.

Phase Three: Bloc Power — When Numbers Become Influence

By the time an enclave reaches a certain size—large enough to sustain its own markets, its own internal economy, its own school preferences, and its own civic priorities—political transformation becomes inevitable. Not sudden. Not dramatic. But inevitable.

Most Americans assume political power is shaped by ideas, debates, or policies. But in identity-based communities, political power flows from cohesion. The individual citizen weighs candidate A versus candidate B; the bloc weighs identity versus identity. And the bloc always wins.

This is how Minneapolis elected Ilhan Omar. Her platform did not rise because Minneapolis as a whole embraced her ideology; it rose because the enclave in her district voted with unity and intensity.

The same dynamic unfolded in Hamtramck, Michigan—once a Polish Catholic enclave, now home to the first all-Muslim city council in the United States. The shift was not ideological; it was demographic. The previous population aged, dispersed, and lost cohesion. The incoming population grew, concentrated, and voted as a unit.

Dearborn followed the same path. As the Muslim population expanded through both intentional migration and high fertility rates, political identity hardened. The election of Abdullah Hammoud as mayor was not a surprise to anyone tracing the demographic curves. His victory was written into the math decades before it was written onto the ballot.

Once bloc power emerges, the civic landscape tilts—not all at once, but perceptibly. The tilt shows up in reliable ways:

- Criticism of policy becomes "Islamophobia."
- Dissent becomes socially punished.
- Civic institutions accommodate rather than negotiate.
- The local press becomes protective rather than investigative.

None of this requires malice. It only requires numbers. When a bloc votes with unity and the surrounding culture votes with fracturing individualism, the outcome is predictable.

Americans were not conquered. They were out-organized.

Bloc power is not the end of the pattern; it is the midpoint. The next stage extends far beyond the original gateway cities, spilling into the surrounding states, counties, and small towns.

And that brings us to Montana.

Phase Four: Secondary Migration — The Quiet Spread Outward

Once an enclave stabilizes in a major metro area, families begin looking outward—not because they reject the city, but because they seek something the enclave can no longer offer: space.

They want larger homes at lower cost.

Safer neighborhoods for children.

Less congestion.

Better schools.

A quieter life still allowing connection to the mother community.

Secondary migration is not random. It follows clear and traceable currents:

- family ties—relatives settling in nearby towns
- mosque networks—satellite congregations expanding from the core
- resettlement organizations—placing new arrivals where housing is available
- nonprofit partnerships—which shape the movement with incentives
- political softness—cities perceived as tolerant, quiet, and accommodating
- university presence—which adds both opportunity and ideological shelter

This is how Minneapolis produced dozens of satellite communities across Minnesota, Wisconsin, and the Dakotas. It is how Columbus reshaped small towns in Ohio. It is how Lewiston, Maine—one of the most unexpected case studies—absorbed thousands of Somali migrants from the upper Midwest. It is how the Pacific Northwest saw its small towns begin to mirror the demographic patterns of Portland and Seattle.

And it is how a line can now be traced from Minneapolis to Missoula. Once the first families establish themselves in a new location, more follow. Once a mosque is planted, the anchor is set. Once the population reaches a certain threshold, the civic recalibration begins.

In Montana terms, it is like seeing the first shoot of knapweed appear in a pasture. The ordinary observer sees a flower. The rancher sees the future.

Secondary migration always leads toward Phase Five. The timeline varies. The conclusion does not.

Interlude: The Kalispell Café Exchange
Fraud, *Taqiyya*, and the Day Minnesota Came to Montana

Introductory Note
December 3, 2025 — Kalispell, Montana
On a cold Wednesday morning in early December, I sat with the men of the Kalispell Café—the same group that gathers every week to trade stories, compare notes on the state of the country, and keep each other rooted in the kind of common sense that once held American life together. The conversation that day turned, as it often does now, to the Somali migration patterns we have been

studying in this chapter—patterns reaching all the way from Minneapolis to Missoula.

What followed around that table became more than small-town talk; it became a living illustration of the very dynamics this chapter seeks to expose. The vignette that follows distills what happened that morning—real men, real frustrations, real clarity—captured as faithfully as memory would allow.

The Kalispell Café Exchange
The Wednesday Coffee Bunch met at the Kalispell Café like we always do—boots dusted from chores, coats draped on the backs of chairs, the smell of bacon and weak diner coffee drifting through the room. The regulars were there: Bill Lincoln leaning back in his chair like the foreman of a construction crew, Ray Thompson stirring his coffee even after the sugar was long dissolved, Roger—quiet and listening, and a handful of older business owners and retirees who've lived long enough to see more than one version of America rise, fall, and try to get up again.

It didn't take long for the topic to find its way to Islam—again. That's not because anyone around that table carries a chip on their shoulder, but because they read the news, they remember history, and they have children and grandchildren whose futures matter.

Bill, who's usually the last one to weigh in on anything theological, broke the seal. "You ever heard of *taqiyya*?" he asked, and the table got quiet.

Bill explained it in the plain way only a Montanan can: a doctrine that allows a Muslim to lie if telling the truth would harm Islam's interest. "Now, I'm not saying every Muslim believes that," he added, "but enough do that you better understand the rules they're playing by."

You could feel a shift. Not anger—clarity. That kind of clarity you only get when someone finally says out loud what everyone else has felt in their bones.

But then Ray jumped in, phone in hand, scrolling through screenshots he'd saved. "Forget abstract theology," he said. "You boys seen what's been going on in Minnesota?" And he held up his phone like a man holding evidence in a courtroom.

There it was in plain text—the timeline of fraud committed by Somali networks in Minnesota, stretching from the early 1990s to today. A billion-dollar welfare racket. "Feeding Our Future"—that was the nonprofit name—a Somali-run organization siphoning off hundreds of millions in taxpayer funds under the guise of feeding kids, when in truth the money was being laundered through Hawala networks, shipped overseas in cash, and funneled into Al-Shabaab and other Islamist operations.

A billion dollars. Not over a decade—in a single year. (And the total promises to go higher.)

Ray zoomed in on one statistic that froze the table: Forty percent of households in Somalia survive on money sent from the Somali diaspora—$1.7 billion per year.

"That's more than their government's entire budget," Ray said. "And guess where a chunk of that comes from? Us. Right here. Montana taxpayers. America's taxpayers. We're not just feeding a broken system—we're financing the very ideology that wants our civilization gone."

Someone muttered, "We're paying for our own funeral."

Another said, "This ain't immigration—it's extraction."

These weren't hotheads. These were men who've worked jobs that tear your hands up, who pay their taxes, who bury their friends and raise their grandkids. Good men. And they were angry—not at immigrants, not at people fleeing war, but at a government so naïve, so morally confused, so utterly unwilling to defend its own people that it became complicit in its own fleecing.

The Department of Justice had already confirmed it—millions siphoned into terrorist networks. Organized fraud. Welfare as a funding pipeline. And every time investigators got close, the perpetrators hid behind the same shields: Racism. Islamophobia. Discrimination. Harassment.

The same pattern Dr. Gad Saad has warned about. The same pattern we are tracing: moral paralysis masquerading as compassion. Institutions too afraid to enforce law. Officials terrified of being called names. A civilization so unsure of itself that it bends to anyone who speaks forcefully enough.

And around that table in Kalispell, no one bought the idea that this was just "Minnesota's problem." Because they'd already seen the pattern drift westward—secondary migration, resettlement networks, nonprofit machinery, seeded enclaves. They'd seen Missoula light up in the same way Minneapolis once did: the same partnerships, the same rhetoric, the same playbook.

Bill shook his head. "You watch," he said. "Montana's next. You get enough people who don't share your values—who think deception is honorable and fraud is justified if it serves the cause—you'll lose the state before you even know it happened."

There wasn't any bravado around the table. Just the kind of sober realization that settles on men who've lived long enough to know how quickly things can fall apart. And the unspoken questions hovered over the group like Montana snow clouds before a storm:

What happens when the moral clarity of Kalispell collides with the immoral calculus of Mogadishu?

What happens when a town built on handshakes, honor, and personal responsibility collides with a worldview built on clan loyalty, opportunism, and religious sanction for deception?

Fraud is not the worst part. It's the motive behind it. It's the worldview that justifies it. It's the governments that protect it.

And it's the quiet Americans who end up paying for it—in dollars at first, in freedoms later. The irritation they felt wasn't abstract. It was personal. You could hear it in their voices: "They reached into my pocket."

And that's the pivot most Americans never make until a moment like this. They think Islamism is distant—a geopolitical storm happening "over there." Then they wake up to find:

- ***The fraud happened in Minnesota.***
- ***The money came from Montana.***

The perpetrators were operating inside the legal and cultural frameworks Americans built and funded. The behavior wasn't an aberration—it operated on the same civilizational assumptions it has operated on for 1,400 years.

And here's the thing our Coffee Bunch felt instinctively: Fraud on that scale isn't just about money. It's about worldview. It's about the difference between a society built on covenantal trust—the residual Christian ethic—and a system built on tribal loyalty, opportunism, and the moral permissions embedded in the Mecca–Medina paradigm.

When a group believes:

- It owes loyalty first to clan, not to country,
- It owes obedience to Sharia, not to civil law,
- It can use deception (*taqiyya, kitman*) for advantage,
- It views non-Muslim money as fair game,
- It considers the host society decadent, gullible, and ripe…

…then why wouldn't they defraud the system when the opportunity is handed to them on a silver platter?

This is not slander; this is history repeating itself—from seventh-century Medina to twenty-first-century Minneapolis.

And here's the deeper truth we carried out of that coffee shop:

Christianity creates a culture where truth-telling is a virtue.

Islamism creates a culture where deception can be a virtue.

Christianity elevates personal responsibility.

Islamism elevates communal advantage.

Christianity forms a conscience before God.

Islamism forms a loyalty to the *ummah*—global Islam.

Those men felt it before they understood it.

We finished our coffee in silence. Not because we were defeated, but because clarity brings weight. And weight brings resolve.

We left the diner knowing this: If Montana pretends this is someone else's story, Montana will become someone else's story. And the men around that table—businessmen, truckers, construction guys, retirees—understood something Washington has forgotten:

A civilization that refuses to defend itself will not be a civilization for long.

Phase Five: Dominance — The Medina Reflex and the Shift of Civic Norms

The final phase is the one Americans struggle most to comprehend because it breaks their categories. They assume democracy is governed by debate, persuasion, and the interchange of ideas. They assume that diversity naturally produces mutual tolerance.

They assume that the West's commitments to free speech, public neutrality, and equal civic space are universally shared. Phase Five proves otherwise.

When an enclave becomes the dominant force in a locality—through demographic concentration, bloc voting, and institutional influence—the civic norms begin to shift from pluralism toward identity-based dominance.

The shift is not always violent. But it is always decisive.

Nowhere is this clearer than in the Mecca–Medina pattern itself:

- In Mecca, Islam asked for tolerance.
- In Medina, Islam demanded submission.

And Islamism today uses Mecca tactics to gain Medina power.

Dearborn, Michigan, offers the clearest American example. When a Christian citizen raised objections to a street being named after a figure with known Islamist ties, the mayor did not respond with debate or explanation. He responded with humiliation—public shaming, moral condemnation, and a declaration that the city would celebrate the day that citizen left town.

That is not pluralism. That is Medina reflex—civilizational dominance expressed through civic authority.

When residents complained about early-morning calls to prayer violating noise ordinances, the city did not revisit or enforce its existing laws. Instead, it treated the complaints as bigotry and allowed religious preference to override municipal regulation.

Law bent.

Identity prevailed.

The pattern completed.

Hamtramck tells the same story in miniature. Once the Muslim population gained political control, the city council banned Pride flags from public property—not from a biblical moral vision, but from Islamic doctrine. The same activists who celebrated Hamtramck as a triumph of diversity suddenly discovered they had empowered a worldview that would not bow to theirs.

What outsiders interpret as inconsistency is simply the outworking of a worldview that places divine law above civic law. What Americans call hypocrisy, Islamists call faithfulness.

This is how the Medina reflex works:
- public criticism becomes morally unacceptable
- religious practice shapes public policy
- objection becomes an act of hostility
- dissenters feel pressured to relocate
- the remaining population adjusts to avoid conflict

When Phase Five arrives, the transformation is complete—not the violent overthrow Americans imagine, but the slow realignment of civic life around the dominant community's norms.

Dearborn is the full-grown tree.
Hamtramck is a branch.
Missoula is the seed.

Missoula is not at Phase Five. But Missoula is on the same road. Missoula is just the beginning of Dearborn tomorrow—if the church and civic leaders repeat the same mistakes.

The pattern does not skip the quiet towns simply because they are smaller. It simply arrives later.

Part III: Migration Without Assimilation — From OIC to U.S. Soil

To see how wide this pattern stretches, you have to pull back from individual cities and look at the map of the Islamic world itself.

The Organisation of Islamic Cooperation (OIC) is a confederation of fifty-six or fifty-seven countries with majority Muslim populations. At one time, every one of those countries had zero Muslims. Now everyone is dominated by Islam. Each was captured over time—some by force, others by stealth and dissimulation. The method varied. The end state did not.

Islam does not drift. It advances. It waits. And when secular power collapses, Islamism steps in.

What has changed in the modern era is not the goal but the available methods. Modern Islamists no longer need armies to invade the West. They use the tools of openness:

- immigration
- refugee pipelines
- birthrates
- social welfare systems
- Western guilt
- religious liberty statutes
- multiculturalism
- political correctness
- fear of offending minorities
- demographic blocs

These are not random tactics. They are modern iterations of the Mecca phase—buying time, building numbers, and constructing parallel societies—until the Medina posture becomes possible.

When we trace the streams of Muslim immigration into the United States over the last half-century, the picture becomes unmistakable. The United States has received immigrants, refugees, and asylum-seekers from well over twenty nations in the OIC—countries stretching from North Africa to the Middle East, Central Asia to Southeast Asia.

The largest streams came from:
- Pakistan
- Bangladesh
- Indonesia
- Turkey
- Egypt
- Iraq
- Iran
- Somalia
- Sudan
- Afghanistan
- Lebanon
- Yemen

These are not isolated pockets on the map; they are the core population centers of the modern Islamic world. Each carries its own history, sectarian tensions, cultural patterns, and interpretations of Islamic law. Yet when settled in the West, these differences tend to dissolve into a single shared identity: Muslim—and therefore distinct from the surrounding secular or Christian culture.

Smaller but significant communities have flowed from Syria, Eritrea, Djibouti, Libya, Morocco, Algeria, and Tunisia. These nations, though diverse in ethnicity and language, share Islamic heritage and often Islamic governance. Their migrants bring patterns of communal cohesion shaped in environments where religion is not a private matter but a public ordering principle.

Add to these streams students and professionals from Jordan, Kuwait, the UAE, Saudi Arabia, Qatar, Oman, and Malaysia—

many of whom arrive temporarily but stay permanently—and you begin to see the breadth of the Islamic world represented within American borders.

But understanding the source countries is only half the picture. The second half is geography—where these populations settled once they arrived. They did not disperse evenly across the country.

They clustered. They gravitated to places where federal resettlement agencies, sympathetic city governments, large universities, and nonprofit networks created a "soft landing zone." That is why...

- Detroit–Dearborn,
- Minneapolis–St. Paul,
- Northern Virginia, and
- the New York–New Jersey corridor

...became the big four enclaves.

Each city offered more than jobs; it offered ecosystems—halal markets, bilingual services, legal advocacy, political platforms, and social networks strong enough to maintain identity without assimilation. From these epicenters, secondary clusters grew:

- Columbus
- Buffalo
- Houston
- Dallas
- Seattle

In each case, the pattern was the same. Once an enclave reached critical mass—once mosques multiplied and cultural boundaries solidified—families began relocating outward to quieter places, places with lower housing costs and higher tolerance for multicultural rhetoric.

That is how Lewiston, Willmar, St. Cloud, Sioux Falls, Boise, and now Missoula entered the story. These are not random dots on the map. They are the second ring of a well-documented migration pattern:
gateway cities → enclaves → secondary migration → political consolidation → cultural transformation.

And here is where the math matters.

Islamic immigration grows not primarily through conversion but through childbirth. Early marriages, large families, tight cultural retention, and multigenerational households create demographic momentum that Western nations—with below-replacement fertility—cannot match.

When a community averages three or four children per household, while the surrounding culture averages between 1.5 and 1.8, the long-term outcome is not speculation. It is arithmetic.

Civilizations shift through infants long before they shift through arguments. And when these communities come from nations where Islam is the public law, not private belief, they often carry expectations shaped by majority status. In Pakistan, Egypt, Iraq, Sudan, Afghanistan, and Somalia, Islamic norms govern marriages, gender relations, public expression, religious freedom, and civic order.

When migrants from these societies arrive in the West, they do not suddenly develop Western assumptions about free speech, religious pluralism, or the primacy of individual conscience. Instead, they often expect the surrounding culture to adjust—to accommodate dietary laws, gender distinctions, prayer times, public calls to worship, and eventually legal or political norms.

What looks like cultural confidence from the inside can feel like cultural pressure from the outside.

Dearborn and Hamtramck are not anomalies. They are case

studies. They demonstrate what happens when migration from multiple OIC countries combines with high fertility, strong cultural retention, and political cohesion. Bloc voting emerges. Parallel society forms. And once a demographic threshold is crossed, the expectation of accommodation becomes an expectation of deference.

What seventh-century Arabia established, and what Islamic jurisprudence preserved, is now visible in twenty-first-century Michigan.

Parallel societies do not stay parallel. They eventually compete. And when they compete, one will dominate.

Part IV: The Montana Imperative — Why Missoula Matters Now

Montana is not the first place people think of when they picture cultural upheaval. Our reputation is built on big sky, big land, and big personal space. We are a state of solitude—mountain passes, ranch gates, quiet valleys, and towns where men still tip their hats and neighbors keep an eye on each other's fences. A sense of moral gravity is here, a kind of American memory that lingers in the pine-scented air long after other regions have forgotten it.

But the story that is unfolding in Missoula is a reminder that no place is too far, too quiet, or too insulated to feel the tremors of global change. And those tremors are already here. They do not look dramatic. They do not look threatening. In fact, they look almost benign. A handful of new families. A shift in a neighborhood. A nonprofit hosting welcome events. A university applauding its own diversity metrics. Each moment seems small, trivial even.

But history is made of accumulations, not single events.

And Missoula is accumulating something that Montanans must not ignore. Missoula is not Dearborn today. But Missoula is the beginning of Dearborn tomorrow.

Not because anyone intends harm. Not because every Muslim migrant seeks political influence. Not because diversity is inherently dangerous. But because patterns have consequences, and those consequences follow the same trajectory wherever certain conditions exist.

Missoula has those conditions:
- A progressive city council eager to display tolerance.
- A university culture that treats multiculturalism as unquestioned gospel.
- A nonprofit landscape flush with federal dollars.
- Churches reluctant to speak clearly.
- Civic leaders more afraid of accusation than of erosion.
- A population that assumes "it can't happen here."

And layered on top of this is something even more consequential: secondary migration, the quiet spread of families who move outward from established enclaves in Minneapolis, Seattle, or Denver once those communities reach critical mass.

These families are not fleeing oppression. They are seeking opportunity—cheaper housing, safer neighborhoods, and communities unlikely to confront them. They are following family ties, mosque networks, and nonprofit pipelines. And they are doing so with the same generational instinct that has guided Islamic expansion for centuries: steady movement into the softest soil.

Missoula is soft soil.

To say this is not to insult the city. It is to name its vulnerability. Cities built on ideology rather than conviction are always the easiest to shape. Cities proud of their tolerance are always the first to be exploited by those who interpret tolerance as weakness. And cities that silence their churches will always discover that other belief systems—stronger, clearer, and more assertive—will fill the vacuum.

Missoula is not falling. It is forming.

Montana stands at the earliest edge of this pattern. But early edges are the critical ones. Because once the growth curve tips, communities have only two choices: confront reality or be shaped by it.

And here is where the Christian dimension becomes unavoidable. If the church stays silent, Islamism will speak. If pastors avoid clarity, imams will fill the moral space. If believers retreat into private faith, public life will be shaped by those who do not. If Christian fathers assume their children inherit Western values by osmosis, they will be stunned to discover that cultural inheritance requires active stewardship.

Montana still has time. As do many communities across the United States.

But time is not neutral. It runs in one direction. It favors those who act, not those who wait. It rewards those who build, not those who assume.

You cannot resist a movement you refuse to name. You cannot prepare for a future you pretend will not arrive. You cannot preserve a culture you are unwilling to defend.

Missoula is the seed.

Dearborn is the tree.

America is the orchard.

And Montana is the open field where the next row may be
    planted.

The question is not whether the seed will sprout. It is whether Montana or your state or region will see the sprout in time.

And the deeper question—the one that sits beneath every other—is this: Will we rediscover enough cultural and spiritual conviction to stand before the branches grow overhead?

Because the future of this state or your state and cities...and the future of small towns like Missoula, Kalispell, Bozeman, and Billings, will not be shaped by the loudest opinions or the latest trends. It will be shaped by whether ordinary people—pastors, fathers, mothers, citizens—discern the tremor beneath their feet and decide, before it is too late, that the inheritance entrusted to them is worth protecting.

That is the imperative. And it begins not tomorrow, not next year, not when the problem becomes obvious. It begins now.

8

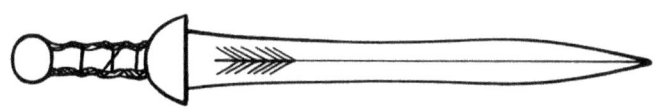

The Deadly Embrace
Pathological Empathy and the Suicidal West

Every civilization develops not only armies and borders, but something far more important: an internal immune system. This is the moral clarity and cultural resolve that allows a people to recognize danger when it approaches, to name it honestly, and to resist it before resistance becomes too costly.

For centuries, the West possessed such an immune system. It was imperfect, sometimes misdirected, but it existed. It drew from the deep well of biblical anthropology, from the conviction that evil is real, that human nature is rebellious and easily corrupted, and that vigilance is not hatred but stewardship.

Today that immune system is failing. And as with any body under attack, death often follows when the infection reaches the heart. If we expect to live, the immune system must be restored.

This chapter examines not Islamism — we did that in Chapter 7 — but the psychological and spiritual condition of the modern West that makes Islamism's advance possible. The greatest threat to America is not merely the ideology pressing in from without, but the inability of our society to recognize that ideology for what it is. While Chapter 7 showed what Islamism does, this chapter explains why the West lets it.

Islamists, historically speaking, have always pressed forward. That is what civilizational ideologies do. The more sobering question is why the West now meets that pressure with apology, confusion, self-censorship, and even admiration. Why do the very groups who would be the first to lose their freedoms under Islamic rule fight the hardest to defend its presence in the West?

The answer lies in a cultural pathology Dr. Gad Saad calls **pathological empathy** — the emotional impulse to protect the predator at the expense of the prey, to embrace the viper as a proof of one's own virtue. It is compassion disconnected from discernment and it is dissolving the West from the inside out.

The Auto-Immune Collapse of the West

A healthy society maintains boundaries — moral, cultural, civic, and spiritual. These boundaries are not walls of hatred; they are necessary definitions of who we are, what we believe, and what we will defend.

But the modern West has been trained for decades to see boundaries as oppressive, distinctions as discriminatory, and judgment as the ultimate sin. The result is an auto-immune disorder, a civilization attacking its own mechanisms of protection in the name of tolerance.

We see this in the growing fear of speaking obvious truths. Ordinary citizens whisper what their grandparents would have said out loud. Pastors avoid passages of Scripture that once formed the backbone of moral clarity. Politicians tiptoe through every issue with the dread of being labeled intolerant. Bureaucracies contort themselves to avoid offense, often enforcing rules that contradict common sense simply to avoid public embarrassment.

Islamism did not create these weaknesses. It merely saw

them — and stepped through the door.

Dr. Saad describes these cultural vulnerabilities as **idea pathogens** — mental habits that make clear thinking almost impossible. Among them are the belief that all cultures are morally equivalent, that every grievance demands apology, that those who claim victimhood possess moral authority, and that truth should never challenge feelings.

This psychological framework is the soil in which Islamism's Western success grows. The threat is not first strategic; it is spiritual. A civilization unwilling to name its own beliefs cannot defend them.

The Illusion of the Protected Class

One of the strangest phenomena of our age is the alliance between progressive identities and Islamist ideology. Every year, activists march for LGBTQ+ rights while waving the flags of movements that would imprison — or execute — them. Feminist leaders publicly defend religious codes that would veil, silence, and diminish them. Secular Jewish organizations defend those chanting for Israel's destruction. Professors invoke academic freedom to protect ideologies that would ban their books and jail their colleagues.

The logic seems to be: "We understand marginalization. You are marginalized too. Therefore, we are allies."

But Islamic law does not recognize protected classes as the West defines them. Under Sharia — historically, legally, and doctrinally — identity groups have no standing apart from their submission or resistance to Islamic authority. The question is not "What gender, race, or orientation are you?" but "Will you submit to Allah's law?"

And if not, history is painfully clear about the consequences.

- There are no pride parades in Gaza.

- No feminist rallies in Tehran.
- No DEI training centers in Mogadishu.
- No transgender sanctuaries in Riyadh.

The very activists who champion tolerance at home would lose every freedom they cherish under the ideology they now defend. They see Islamists as oppressed cousins in a shared struggle against Western "hegemony," when in truth they are temporary allies in a movement far older and far more serious than the language of intersectionality can grasp.

The West's most fragile minds are protecting the movements that would end them. This is not alliance; it is delusion — a temporary truce in which only one side intends a future.

The Safe Viper Illusion

Another form of delusion grows from the West's obsession with empathy. For generations, Western children have been taught that the highest moral good is kindness without judgment, compassion without discernment, affirmation without limits.

This produces a predictable belief: "If I am kind to the viper, the viper will be kind to me."

Modern Western elites — professors, journalists, activists, bureaucrats — assume that empathy can tame every passion, disarm every ideology, and re-write every ancient conviction. But Islamism does not read kindness as compassion. It reads it as weakness, as an opportunity, as confirmation that the host society lacks the will to enforce its own norms.

The early Islamic sources praise strategy, concealment, patience, and advantage — principles that make perfect sense in the struggle for religious dominance. To a civilization built on conquest and governed by divine mandate, the soft-hearted confusion of the West is not admirable; it is exploitable.

This is not bigotry. This is anthropology. And anthropology, unlike ideology, does not lie.

The Fantasy of Shared Victimhood

A further confusion arises in the assumption that "oppressed groups" naturally form alliances. Because the modern West interprets nearly everything through the lens of power dynamics, it assumes that any movement opposed to Western norms must be part of a common resistance.

Thus, feminists assume Islamists share their anger at patriarchy; LGBTQ+ activists assume Islamists share their desire for liberation; secular humanists assume Islamists share their suspicion of traditional Christianity.

But these assumptions reflect Western grievances, not Islamic convictions. Islamism is not seeking liberation from Western structures. It is seeking the replacement of Western structures. The "alliance" is temporary, built on illusion. It is the old Middle Eastern proverb: **"The enemy of my enemy is my friend."** Until the moment that friend no longer serves the cause.

History is full of such alliances — and the smaller, weaker party is always the first to be sacrificed.

The Guilt-Driven Conscience of the West

If you trace Western political discourse over the last fifty years, you will see a steady erosion of civilizational confidence. Every institution has internalized the belief that the West's achievements are built on exploitation, that prosperity is suspect, that strength is oppressive, and that the burden of history must be paid through self-abnegation.

This moral exhaustion produces a reflexive guilt that misreads aggression as victimhood and treats assertiveness as a cry for help. A fraudulent welfare network in Minnesota is excused as an issue of "equity." A coordinated migration bloc is celebrated as diversity. A religious ideology with global conquest in its DNA is treated as a misunderstood cousin of Western pluralism.

Dr. Saad calls this **empathetic suicide** — a civilization proving its goodness by dissolving its survival instinct. Islamists do not find this strategy confusing. They find it useful. They have encountered it many times before.

The Myth of Endless Pluralism

Pluralism is a noble experiment, perhaps the best the West has ever attempted. But it is also a fragile one. It presupposes a shared moral groundwork — the dignity of the individual, the freedom of conscience, the equality of all citizens under law.

But Islamism contains within itself a different vision of society. In Islamic jurisprudence, peace is not the coexistence of differing convictions. Peace is the state that prevails once the will of Allah is established.

The West assumes pluralism is permanent.

Islamism assumes pluralism is a temporary condition.

And when two missionary civilizations share a single civic square, only one can ultimately define the space.

And just to be sure, we are not speaking here about every Muslim neighbor or coworker. Many Muslims ache for freedom, resent corruption, and quietly suffer under the same ideologies we are describing.

The historical record makes the ambitions of radical Islamism difficult to deny. According to data from the French think tank *Fondation Pour l'Innovation Politique* (Fondapol), there were at least 66,872 Islamic terrorist attacks worldwide between February 1979 and April 2024, resulting in at least 249,941 deaths. The majority of victims of Islamic terrorism are themselves Muslims. Radical Islamists are focused on total submission. And that applies to other Muslims as well as the infidels.

Our concern is not with individual Muslims as people — many of whom would welcome the very freedoms the West is losing. Our concern is with Islamism as a political-theological project that uses them—and us—for its ends.

The Church's Confusion: Compassion Without Clarity
Finally, the surrender of the West cannot be explained without naming the particular failure of the Christian church. A generation of pastors, eager to avoid controversy and terrified of seeming intolerant, have softened the biblical categories of good and evil until they are indistinguishable. They preach a Jesus who comforts but does not confront, who forgives but never warns, who welcomes but never watches.

This therapeutic Christianity produces people who believe that all conflict is unchristlike, all distinctions are prideful, and all vigilance is a failure of love.

> But Jesus spoke often of wolves. He warned of deception. He confronted false shepherds.
> Paul confronted false teachers with clarity and courage.
> Peter warned of destructive heresies.
> John told the church to "test the spirits."

Compassion without discernment is not Christlike. It is dangerous. Our therapeutic preachers would do well to recall the whole counsel of God. In the same verse where Paul promotes love, he also urges hatred of evil: *Love is to be sincere and active [the real thing—without guile and hypocrisy]. Hate what is evil [detest all ungodliness, do not tolerate wickedness]; hold on tightly to what is good* (Rms. 12:9 Amplified Bible).

When Christian leaders fail to speak with clarity, the flock mistakes quietness for safety. They assume that silence equals peace. They forget that wolves are most successful when shepherds have lost their voice.

Why Islamism Cannot Be Managed

Bureaucrats and activists in the West operate under the assumption that every deep conflict can be resolved through dialogue, diversity seminars, or financial programs. They imagine Islamism to be a misunderstanding, a cultural grievance, an identity expression that needs affirmation.

But Islamism is not asking to be affirmed. It is announcing what it intends to become. It is not a movement seeking equal space. It is a movement seeking final space.

You cannot negotiate with a civilizational claim.

You cannot manage a theology of supremacy.

You cannot bureaucratize an eschatology.

You cannot appease an ideology that interprets appeasement as surrender.

History is merciless toward civilizations that forget these truths. But history is not the only judge. The church must answer to Christ for what she does in moments like this.

A Call to the Church

In the end, the survival of the West will not be determined in legislatures or at ballot boxes, but in pulpits and in the quiet work of local congregations learning again how to think theologically about the age in which they live. No civilization can remain free if its churches lose the courage to speak clearly. And no people can discern truth if those entrusted with the Word of God refuse to name the forces that shape the world their children will inherit.

Three imperatives rise from the rubble of Western confusion.

First, the church must recover doctrinal clarity.
For a generation, many pulpits have traded biblical precision for therapeutic uplift. The result is a Christianity too thin to resist the pressures of a missionary ideology like Islamism, and too timid to confront the moral confusion of the West.

When pastors stop preaching sin, judgment, truth, and the lordship of Christ, their people lose the categories they need to recognize deceit when it enters the public square. Doctrinal clarity is not a luxury; it is a shield. Without it, congregations become soft targets for every cultural wind that blows.

Second, the church must teach its people the difference between love and capitulation.
Modern sentimentality has convinced many Christians that kindness requires agreement, that compassion requires silence, and that disagreement is somehow unchristlike. But Jesus loved sinners without ever affirming their sin.

Paul confronted falsehood because love demands it. The church must recover this moral spine. To love our Muslim neighbors, we must refuse the ideologies that enslave them. To love our own children, we must equip them to stand against the lies that shape their world. Love without truth is not love at all. It is surrender dressed in virtue's clothing.

Third, the church must refuse to outsource civilizational discernment to secular elites.
Academia, media, and political institutions have proven unable — and often unwilling — to tell the truth about Islamism, cultural decline, or moral disorder. Their frameworks are too compromised by ideology and too fragile to withstand accusations of intolerance.

When the church looks to these institutions to define compassion, justice, or truth, it inherits their blindness. Pastors must lead again, without apology. They must teach their people how to evaluate cultural movements, political narratives, and global ideologies through the lens of Scripture rather than the vocabulary of the age.

These are not optional tasks. They are matters of stewardship and survival.

If the church regains her clarity, the West has a fighting chance. If she does not, no political movement or cultural campaign will save her.

The moment demands courage. The gospel supplies it. And the world — including millions of Muslims longing for true freedom — is waiting for a church that knows the difference between compassion and compromise, between truth and illusion, between peace and the silent advance of a lie.

The Conclusion: *The Viper and the Hand That Cradles It*

Chapter 7 showed how Islamism advances. This chapter shows why the West is unable — or unwilling — to resist that advance.

What conquers the West will not be the viper alone, but the hand that cradles it, the heart that refuses to believe vipers exist, and the mind that mistakes the tightening coils for an embrace.

- Islamism thinks in centuries.
- The West thinks in sentiments.

And unless the church recovers its clarity, unless citizens recover their courage, unless leaders recover their confidence, America will continue to follow the path of every civilization that believed its ideals could survive without its spine.

The danger is not only the ideology pressing against our gates. It is the moral confusion that keeps the gates open and the silence of the shepherds who should have been standing watch.

INTERLUDE
Christianity and Islam

It was close to midnight at a Waffle House off the interstate—the kind of place where the light is sharp, the coffee is strong, and the conversation grows oddly honest when the hour is late and the day has been long. I had been immersed for hours in the swirl of Islamic history—Mecca to Medina, Qur'an to Hadith, caliphates to modern jihadism—and my mind was still sorting through the debris of centuries.

My friend, Ivan, slid into the booth across from me, weary from his own long day pulling the second shift. We had been looking into the origins and belief system of Islam. It had been saturating the news—really for decades. But recent developments had piqued our interest. After a few pleasantries and his order had been placed, he asked the question that had been troubling him: *"Charles, when you cut through all the noise, what are the real differences between Christianity and Islam? Not stereotypes, not talking points — the documented, historical differences?"*

I didn't answer at first. Some questions deserve a pause, a moment of reflection. I took a sip of coffee, felt the heat, and reached for a napkin. The waitress stopped by, topped off the cup, and left us to our thoughts.

"Let's make a list," I finally said. "Let's get it down clean."

And there, on those thin paper napkins, we began sketching the contrasts — not to mock, not to condemn, not to stoke hostility — but to name the differences honestly so that Christians, pastors, and citizens alike might see the world with clarity. What emerged wasn't speculation or rhetoric. It was history. It was stated and dictated theology. It was lived reality across continents and centuries.

And as we wrote, the contrasts sharpened.

The Character of God

In Christianity, God is revealed as Father — relational, covenantal, knowable through Christ.

In Islam, Allah is Master — distant, will-driven, unknowable except through decrees.

As I told my friend, *relationship shapes one faith; submission structures the other.*

Truth and Revelation

Christian revelation flows from God's unchanging character — truth is stable.

Islamic revelation includes abrogation — later verses override earlier ones.

For Christians, truth is anchored.

For Islam, truth shifts with circumstance.

The Model of the Founder

Jesus never wielded a sword.

Muhammad wielded many.

Jesus forgave His enemies.

Muhammad conquered His.

What the founder is, the movement becomes. History bears that out.

The Nature of Salvation
Christianity rests on grace — God acting to save humanity through Christ.
Islam rests on works — deeds weighed on a scale with no assurance of acceptance.
One gives peace with God.
The other offers perpetual uncertainty.

The Human Person
Christianity teaches *imago Dei* — every person possessing intrinsic dignity.
Islam assigns dignity hierarchically — Muslim male at the top, non-Muslim female at the bottom.
One elevates universally.
The other stratifies socially.

The View of Women
Christianity honors women as equal bearers of God's image.
Islamic law (in its classical form) devalues women legally and socially.
This isn't prejudice. This isn't caricature. It's codified law in classical Islamic jurisprudence.

The Ethics of Violence
Christianity carries no mandate for forced conversion.
Islam sanctions jihad as a legitimate means of advancing the faith.
One spreads by persuasion.
The other has historically spread by conquest.

The State and the Sword

Christianity distinguishes God's kingdom from Caesar's government.

Islam merges mosque and state — religion *is* law, law *is* religion.

Where Christianity allowed pluralism, Islam institutionalized Sharia.

Enemies and Outsiders

Christ calls believers to love their enemies.

The Qur'an calls believers to subjugate them.

The difference is not abstract. It produces dramatically different civilizations.

The Ethics of Deception

Christian faith demands truth because God is truth.

Islam permits deception in specific circumstances to protect or advance the faith.

In one worldview, truthfulness is a virtue.

In the other, strategy sometimes supersedes honesty.

History's Destination

Christianity waits on the return of Christ — the Kingdom arriving by God's act.

Islam works toward the world's submission to Islamic law before the final judgment.

One faith anticipates a King.

The other prepares dominion.

Conversion and Conscience
Christianity insists on freedom of conscience.
Islam often punishes apostasy.
The difference between persuasion and coercion is the difference between liberty and fear.

The Conversation That Followed
As we finished the list, my friend sat back in the booth, hands folded around the warm mug.

"So the differences aren't minor," he finally said.

"No," I told him. "They run to the roots — theology, ethics, authority, power, human dignity, the meaning of freedom. These distinctions shape entire cultures. They shape laws. They shape what kind of society emerges wherever each faith gains influence."

He nodded. "And we pretend they don't matter."

"We pretend," I said, "until the consequences arrive."

Outside, the Waffle House sign hummed. Trucks rolled by on the interstate, their headlights streaking across the windows. It struck me that the contrast we had drawn on paper napkins was the story of history itself. Two visions of God, man, and society moving across centuries, sometimes peacefully, often violently, now meeting again on Western soil. Not as abstractions, but as competing civilizational forces.

This wasn't fearmongering. It wasn't hostility. It was clarity — the clarity Martha Jo saw in 1979, the clarity the West has avoided ever since. She was right: *"Islam is the scariest thing I have ever encountered... a threat to all of Christendom."*

Not because Muslims are our enemies. But because the theology, ethics, and trajectory of Islam differ so radically from the gospel that built the Western world.

And if we fail to understand those differences — if we hide them under sentiment, or euphemisms, or political slogans — we will lose the clarity needed to stand.

The diner had grown quiet by then. The hour was late. The plates were empty. The coffee was gone. But the truth remained — scribbled across a few napkins, waiting to be told to a church and a nation that desperately need to hear it.

"Come on," I finally said as we slid out of the booth. "We've got work to do."

The Ambassador's Statement to Jefferson

In March 1786, when Thomas Jefferson and John Adams met in London with **Sidi Haji Abdul Rahman Adja**, the ambassador of **Tripoli**, they asked him why the Barbary states were attacking American ships that had never provoked them.

The ambassador answered with a candor that shocked even the diplomats of the Enlightenment. His answer was blunt, unembarrassed, and entirely theological:

"It was written in our Qur'an that all nations who had not acknowledged the Prophet were sinners, whom it was the right and duty of the faithful to plunder and enslave; and that every Muslim who was slain in this warfare was sure to go to Paradise."

Jefferson's Response

Jefferson came away from that meeting with one conclusion:

You cannot negotiate with an ideology that sees you as lawful prey.

That is why, once he became president, he refused to continue the European custom of paying tribute, and instead sent the

U.S. Navy and Marine Corps to break the Barbary extortion system. The First Barbary War (1801–1805) was the United States' first major foreign military campaign — and it was undertaken *because* of that worldview clash.

Jefferson understood at once what many Western leaders still refuse to admit today:

Some ideologies do not negotiate — they advance.

There *is* one more layer worth noting — a layer that ties Jefferson's moment to *our* moment with startling clarity. And it is this:

Jefferson didn't just learn something about Islam. He learned something about *civilizations*— his and theirs.

Many Americans know the quote from the Tripolitan ambassador, but very few understand what Jefferson concluded about it. It wasn't merely that Islam had a doctrine of jihad. That was well known among European powers. Jefferson grasped something deeper — something every wise statesman in every generation must hold fast:

A civilization that forgets the convictions its enemies live by will eventually be ruled by them.

Three Additional Insights Jefferson Carried Forward

You may want these on the record, because they speak right into the heart of Chapters 6 and 7 — and into the heart of America's current amnesia.

1. Jefferson realized that America's ideals were powerless without American resolve.

He believed in liberty, individual rights, and the natural equality of mankind.

But the ambassador taught him something he had not fully confronted:

There are adversaries who do not care about your ideals.

There are worldviews that do not meet you on the ground of mutual respect.

There are people who interpret mercy as weakness and negotiation as surrender.

Jefferson's conclusion?

"Weakness provokes insult and injury."

In other words: **If a people will not defend their freedoms, their enemies will define their future.** That is exactly the mistake the West is making today.

2. Jefferson recognized that Islam's political theology was incompatible with republican government.
He tried—briefly—to understand the Barbary perspective. He asked questions. He read their texts. He wanted to see if reason or diplomacy could bridge the gap.

It couldn't.

Why?

Because *Sharia is not merely a religious code*. It is a full civilizational blueprint — legal, political, social, economic.

Jefferson realized what Europe had known for centuries:
- In Christianity, religion and state are distinct.
- In Islamism, religion and state are one.

Therefore, Islamism can never share the public square as an equal partner with any other worldview. This wasn't prejudice. It was *political physics*:

Two systems cannot occupy the same civic space when one believes it has divine authority to dominate the other.

That truth hasn't changed.

3. Jefferson understood that forgetting a lesson learned in blood always leads to repeating it.
America won the First Barbary War and later the second.
But after the Civil War…
after industrial expansion…
after the world wars…
after prosperity and distraction took hold…

America forgot.

She forgot that some worldviews do not modernize.
She forgot that not every culture is converging on Western values.
She forgot that demographic expansion is more powerful than military conquest.
She forgot that enemies who think in centuries will always outmaneuver nations that think in news cycles.

And today?

She is relearning the same lesson — not from pirates off Tripoli, but from mosques in Minnesota, city councils in Michigan, migration patterns across the West, and political blocs that speak softly until their numbers say otherwise.

The Line That Ties It All Together
"Now, we forget that — and in our loss of memory we will find our subjugation."

That is exactly the warning Jefferson left for us — and exactly the warning this book is sounding.

The Final Word:
Civilizations don't fall in a moment.
　　They fall in the moments when no one thinks they're falling.

It isn't the blast of war that ruins a people first.
It's the long drift before the blast.
It's the soft thinking, the unguarded gates, the wishful illusions.
It's forgetting the lessons that hard men learned in hard times.

And that — that forgetting — is the danger zone America is in at this moment.

9

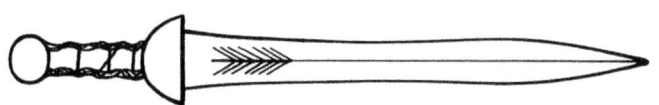

The Silent Siege
Unrestricted Warfare, Digital Tyranny, and the Coming Storm

"The supreme art of war is to subdue the enemy without fighting." —Sun Tzu

We face a civilizational rival whose strategy stretches across centuries rather than election cycles, dynasties rather than presidencies.

China does not shout its intentions from minarets with the fiery sermons of radical Islamism, nor does it march through the institutions as the heirs of Gramsci have done for three generations. It does not rely on immigration, ideological agitation, or cultural infiltration in the traditional sense. China is something different—something older, colder, more calculating, and perhaps the most dangerous of all.

What Marx dreamed, what Gramsci theorized, what Islamism attempts through the womb and parallel societies, China executes through the quiet, deliberate machinery of a centralized state.

If Marxist infiltration rots a nation from within…

If Islamism breaches the walls by demographic pressure…

Then China builds a twenty-story siege tower, wheels it to the gate, and moves under the cover of fog.

China is not the only nation capable of tyranny. But it is the first to construct the most advanced system of digital authoritarianism in the history of humanity. China now stands as the world's first functioning prototype of a Revelation-13 order—an integrated system where buying and selling are controlled, where movement and identity are monitored, where worship is regulated, and where allegiance is tracked by cameras, sensors, algorithms, and state policy.

The persecuted Church in China is not living in a prediction of what may come. They are living in the early operating version of the very thing Christians have expected to come since the Apostle John's revelation on Patmos. That system is now operational.

And the Church must wake up to the reality:
The persecuted Church in China is living today what the Church in the West may face tomorrow.

The Doctrine Behind the Dragon: Unrestricted Warfare

In 1999, two senior PLA colonels—Qiao Liang and Wang Xiangsui—published a book titled *Unrestricted Warfare*. It was not a conspiracy tract or a theoretical exercise in geopolitical speculation. It was a military strategy blueprint, a declaration of intent, and a sober revelation of how China planned to surpass the United States without resorting to conventional conflict.

Their thesis was simple and devastating:
- Modern war is total war.
- Every domain is a battlefield.

- Every system is a weapon.
- Every weakness is an entry point.
- And victory no longer requires bullets.

This was the unveiling of a new category of conflict—war fought with banks instead of bombs, supply chains instead of soldiers, influence operations instead of infantry. It signaled the rise of a cold, quiet, persistent war that operates outside the Geneva conventions and far beneath the threshold of what traditional strategists call conflict. Below is the distilled architecture of their strategy—a framework for defeating America without firing a shot.

Following is the essence of their strategy—China's playbook for defeating America without firing a shot.

China's Fourteen-Front Siege

China does not wage war like the regimes of the past. It does not need tanks, missiles, or marching armies—although it is developing all of these at breakneck speed. Beijing has embraced the doctrine of **unrestricted warfare**—the idea that everything is a weapon and everywhere is a battlefield. Economics, culture, drugs, technology, data, influence, fear—nothing is off limits.

And it does so with the patience of an empire that thinks in centuries, not election cycles.

The strategy unfolds on fourteen fronts. Miss even one, and you won't understand the war that is already underway.

Here is the siege we face.

1. Financial Warfare

Use economic dependency as a weapon. Exploit greed. Manipulate markets. Control critical supply chains. Destabilize the opponent by choking its industries.

China learned a lesson Islamists learned the hard way: blow up America's buildings and the giant awakens. Bleed America's factories and the giant falls asleep.

2. Trade & Industrial Warfare

Steal intellectual property. Force technology transfers. Dump products below market to destroy competitors. Exploit American corporations who worship quarterly profits more than national security.

China observed: America will sell its own birthright for cheaper goods.

3. Media & Cultural Warfare

Suppress unfavorable narratives. Shape Hollywood's portrayals. Pressure companies to self-censor.

Influence universities with funding. Exploit social media algorithms—TikTok is not entertainment: It is psychological warfare disguised as dancing.

4. Cyber Warfare

Hack government agencies. Steal military secrets. Compromise corporations. Penetrate infrastructure. Harvest personal data. Monitor dissidents abroad.

China has stolen more data on Americans than any nation in history. It is building leverage today to apply pressure tomorrow.

5. Legal Warfare ("Lawfare")

Weaponize America's openness. Use our courts against us. Exploit loopholes. Shape global norms favorable to China.

This is Gramsci with Mandarin precision.

6. Psychological Warfare

Destabilize society by amplifying division.

- Left vs. Right
- Black vs. White
- Rich vs. Poor
- Male vs. Female
- Citizen vs. Immigrant

If America hates itself, China wins—without a punch thrown.

7. Fentanyl & Smuggling Warfare
This is not random. Fentanyl precursors are produced in China, shipped to Mexico, Venezuela, and other countries and then flood across our borders. China does not have to invade—it gets others nearer our borders to do it for them. This is chemical warfare through the bloodstream of a nation.

8. Resource Warfare
Control rare earth minerals.
Corner supply chains.
Dominate manufacturing.
Leave America unable to function without Chinese materials.
"When the dragon controls your raw materials, you are already conquered."

9. Infrastructure & Investment Warfare
Use loans, ports, and construction deals to bind nations. The Belt and Road Initiative was China's massive global development strategy launched in 2013 tying the nations of the world to China. Every deal is a chain with a lock.

10. Network Warfare
This is the heart of the dragon.

Surveillance.
Facial recognition.
Biometric tracking.
AI-powered monitoring.
Social credit systems.
Internet filtering.

This is not merely a system—it's a cage with lights off.

11. Proxy Warfare

Support nations hostile to the U.S.: Iran, North Korea, and others. China doesn't need to fire a shot if its proxies bleed America on its behalf.

12. Ecological & Biological Warfare

Disrupt ecosystems.
Compete for water.
Experiment with biological agents: COVID showed how unprepared the world is for biological disruption—intentional or accidental.

13. Space Warfare

Develop anti-satellite weapons.
Disrupt global communication and GPS.
The next war may be fought in orbit.

14. Technological Warfare

AI, quantum computing, hypersonics, 5G systems, drone swarms, supercomputing—these are the realms where and how the dragon intends to leapfrog the eagle.

China's Model: A Prototype of the Beast System

The book of Revelation speaks of a system in which:

- No one can buy or sell without approval
- Identity is controlled
- Allegiance is monitored
- Dissent is punished
- Worship is regulated
- The state claims divine prerogatives
- Technology drives total control

Most Christians read these words and whisper, "It can't happen here."

But China has already built it—operational, scalable, and exportable. Not in theory. Not in allegory. Not in some sci-fi novel. In reality. Right now. At scale.

The Chinese Communist Party has created the first functioning total technocratic surveillance regime in human history. What John saw in prophetic vision, China has built in hardware, software, and law.

The Social Credit System: Revelation 13 in Beta Format

- Every person has a digital profile
- Every action is recorded
- Cameras track movement
- Purchases are monitored
- Messages are screened
- Worship is watched
- Loyalty is measured
- Travel can be restricted
- Bank accounts can be frozen
- Flights can be denied
- Children can be blocked from schools

- Employment can be revoked

All by algorithm. All instantly. All silently. And Christians are targeted first.

Why?

Because Christians bow to no king but Christ. And in China, that is treason.

The Persecuted Church in China: A Glimpse of Our Possible Future

The underground Church in China is not an artifact of old missions newsletters. It is vibrant, courageous, multiplying, and astonishingly resilient. They worship in whispers, evangelize under surveillance, and endure imprisonment, re-education, digital erasure, and the demolition of their church buildings. They are the beating heart of Christian courage in our generation.

What they endure is a preview of what technological authoritarianism could impose on the West.

China is not merely a nation—it is a laboratory. Technologies of oppression never remain isolated. Iran wants them. Russia wants them. Islamists want them. Western elites admire them. And American institutions, intoxicated by power, are often eager to adopt them.

China provides the machinery.
Marxism provides the ideology.
Technocracy provides the method.
Islamism provides the will to dominate.
America provides the naivety.

The wall is not breached by a single enemy, but by a convergence of hostile forces that share one hatred: ***the freedom found in Jesus Christ.***

Why China Fears Christianity

China does not suppress Christians merely because they are religious.

China suppresses Christians because Christians cannot be bought, bribed, intimidated, or subordinated to Caesar. A people who bow to Christ cannot be ruled by the state. That is why China rewrites Scripture, demolishes churches, arrests pastors, and criminalizes unregistered worship.

Because the Cross is the one symbol no authoritarian regime can tolerate.

What This Means for America

The United States is not China. Not yet.

But the scaffolding of control is already under construction:

- AI surveillance
- corporate–government partnerships
- digital financial systems
- speech policing
- travel restrictions
- bureaucratic weaponization
- ideological loyalty tests
- monitoring of religious dissent

The seeds are planted. The soil is ready. And the people remain largely unaware.

China is not simply an external threat—it is a teacher demonstrating what is possible when power, technology, and ideology align.

Conclusion: Watchman, Pastor, Soldier

We end where all true Christian resistance begins—with clarity of calling. In moments like these, God summons His people to stand in their appointed place. Like Gideon's 300, each of us must be found in the battleline leaving no gap for the enemy.

Watchman:

The dragon is not distant. Its tools are not theoretical. Its influence is not foreign. The siege tower is at the gate. And the church must warn a nation willing to trade liberty for convenience and truth for comfort.

Pastor:

Our neighbors, families, and communities are not insulated from this storm. The persecuted church in China calls out to us across oceans and fire: *"Be faithful unto death, and He will give you the crown of life."*

Soldier:

Stand firm. Sharpen your sword. Guard your conscience. Refuse to bow to any system that demands allegiance above Christ.

What our Chinese brothers endure today, we may endure tomorrow. But we face it with the same courage, because the same Christ reigns over all. And having done all—we will stand, each in the place God has called us to hold.

10

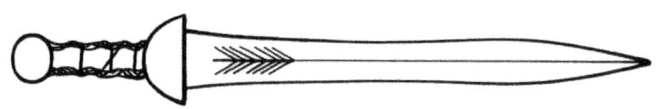

Parasitic Patterns
When the Host Loses Its Center

Every invasion tells two stories—one about the intruder's strategy and one about the host's weakness.

America faces three distinct adversaries—**Gramsci/Frankfurt Marxism, Islamist civilizational expansion, and China's unrestricted warfare**—each different in motive and expression, but identical in method.

They flourish only when the host grows weak and unaware.
- A confident civilization resists infiltration.
- A coherent civilization repels manipulation.
- A morally grounded civilization recognizes danger.
- A hollow civilization does none of these.

And biology gives us a picture of how it happens.

The following examples are not offered for shock value. They are mirrors.

Just as **China quietly placed a spy in Dianne Feinstein's employ for twenty years,**

Just as the **Thousand Talents Program embedded researchers in our universities,**

Just as **Islamist enclaves have created parallel civic structures in Hamtramck, Dearborn, and parts of Texas,**

Just as **Marxist ideology hollowed out schools through DEI bureaucracies and curriculum capture,**

...so these biological strategies reveal a deeper pattern at work.

The Six Behaviors All Parasites Share

Whether in nature or nations, infiltrators operate by the same process:

1. Entry through a weakness
2. Hijacking the host's neurological center
3. Redirecting the host's behavior
4. Building a parallel structure inside the host
5. Using the host's own systems against itself
6. Replacing the host's identity with the parasite's purpose

Marxists use this in universities and bureaucracies.
Islamists use it in enclaves and legal structures.
China uses it in economics, research, and political influence.

Watch how nature reveals the pattern.

1. Ophiocordyceps — The Zombie-Ant Fungus
Identity Lost

In the rainforests of South America, there exists a fungus called Ophiocordyceps — often called the "zombie-ant fungus." It does not kill the ant outright. That would be wasteful. Instead, it performs a far more sophisticated strategy:

Entry Through a Weakness

Ophiocordyceps doesn't attack from strength—it enters quietly through a weakness. A spore lands on an ant. Nothing dramatic. Nothing alarming. Just a little vulnerability at the wrong moment.

China uses the same principle:
it sends students into engineering programs, not with weapons, but with scholarships—quietly embedding operatives who return home with proprietary research, advanced manufacturing processes, and defense-related technology.
No alarms.
Just access.

Hijacking the Neurological Center

Once inside, the fungus doesn't kill the ant. It does something far more chilling. It hijacks the ant's neurological center, rewiring its instincts and overriding its decision-making. The ant thinks it is choosing—but it is being steered.

This is how Marxist capture works.
DEI offices now dictate hiring, speech, and curriculum in universities.
The institution's own "decision-making center"—its academic senate, its HR, its mission—is overridden by a new ideological instinct imposed from within.

Redirecting Behavior

The parasite forces the ant to abandon the colony—its community, its structure, its identity—and climb a nearby plant. At precisely the right height and humidity, the ant clamps down on a leaf vein and freezes. That famous "death grip" is not the ant's choice. It is the parasite's strategy.

So do captured institutions.
Universities that once elevated free inquiry now police speech. Media outlets that once reported truth now curate narratives. School boards follow ideological directives rather than parental authority.

They are climbing—but not by their own choice.

Building a Parallel Structure Inside the Host
Then the real work begins. The fungus grows a parallel structure inside the host, consuming the ant from within while building its own reproductive stalk. The ant's body—its physical shell—serves the parasite's purpose.

Islamist enclaves do the same:
- parallel legal structures (sharia councils),
- parallel schooling,
- parallel banking,
- parallel civic identity.

They do not assimilate into the host culture—they build beside it, inside it, beneath it.

The ant's outside remains an ant. Its inside is something else.

Using the Host Against Itself
Finally, the parasite uses the host against itself: the spore stalk erupts and rains infection down on the colony below. One compromised ant becomes a vector to destroy the whole.

This is China's economic strategy.
Use American supply chains, investment capital, research labs, manufacturing systems—all built by Americans—to strengthen Beijing's global dominance and weaken American independence.

Replacing the Host's Identity
What was once an ant is now a delivery system for something foreign. And the ant's original identity? Gone. Replaced by the parasite's endgame.

And so with nations: symbols remain, institutions remain, structures remain…
…but the inner life of the culture—its meaning, its confidence, its beliefs—has been replaced.

If Ophiocordyceps is <u>horror</u>, the Jewel Wasp is <u>precision</u>.

2. The Emerald Jewel Wasp — The Beautiful Assassin
Will Removed: when the will is removed but the body marches on

The Emerald Jewel Cockroach Wasp uses an equally chilling strategy to the Zombie-Ant Fungus. The wasp looks almost harmless at first glance—a small, iridescent creature native to the tropics of Africa and Asia. But its beauty hides one of the most precise parasitic strategies in nature.

It does not kill the cockroach it targets. It does something far more strategic. ***It disables its will.***

With stunning accuracy, the wasp delivers two injections—the <u>first</u> to weaken the roach's mobility, the <u>second</u> into the exact neurological center that governs the impulse to flee.

The cockroach can still walk, breathe, digest, and function. Its muscles work. Its systems run.

But its instinct to resist is gone. The roach is fully alive…but no longer self-directed.

From there, the wasp simply takes the antenna—like a leash—and leads the still-living host into a burrow it would never choose on its own. The roach walks obediently, quietly, almost peacefully. The will has been removed, but the body marches on.

And what grows inside that host is not a renewed roach—but a new creature born from its surrender.

Note the tactics of this beautiful but highly evolved murderer:

Entry Through a Weakness
The wasp doesn't kill the roach.
It disables the instinct to resist.

This is how America's bureaucratic capture unfolded.
Teachers weren't fired—they were trained in new vocabulary.
Pastors weren't arrested—they were conditioned to avoid "controversy."
Corporations weren't toppled—they were nudged into ESG compliance.

Hijacking the Decision-Making Center
The sting alters the roach's will to flee.

China has done this geopolitically.
American CEOs are not forced to comply—they *choose* to, because access to Chinese markets becomes their leash.

The roach can move.
It just no longer wants to.

Redirecting Behavior
The wasp leads the roach by the antenna into a burrow it would never choose.

So too with captured institutions:
- Universities now follow ideology they once rejected.
- Churches drift into silence on issues Scripture addresses plainly.
- Cities adopt policies whose consequences they can already see in San Francisco or Portland.

They walk into the burrow willingly—but not freely.

Building a Parallel Structure Inside the Host
The wasp lays an egg in the roach.
A new life form grows from within.

Islamist enclaves follow this pattern:
They begin as immigrant communities—then grow into self-contained zones with their own norms, law, identity, and political bloc. Hamtramck, Michigan, was not conquered from outside. It was transformed from within.

Using the Host's Systems Against Itself
The roach's own body sustains the invader's future.

This is China's financial model.
They buy American farmland, ports, factories, and data centers—using America's own assets to undermine American sovereignty.

Replacing the Host's Identity
The roach's form remains. Its identity does not. This is the fate of any institution that yields its center. It becomes a delivery system for a purpose it no longer recognizes.

What we have just seen in nature is not a curiosity. It is a mirror.

If you want to know how this pattern looks in the real world—not in the jungle, but in Washington, Wall Street, and Wuhan—just open your eyes to six places where the parasite is already feeding on the host. And if these images feel extreme, hold that thought.

They are not exaggerations—they are explanations. The same pattern of weakness, capture, redirection, and replacement we saw in the parasitic examples is unfolding in America right now. It is being carried out in boardrooms, laboratories, factories, and the highest levels of American leadership.

1. The Pharmaceutical Stranglehold — America's Medicine in China's Hand

Before 2020, very few Americans realized that **over 85% of our generic drugs—or their active ingredients—are made in China**. Antibiotics, blood pressure meds, diabetes meds, antidepressants, chemotherapy agents—all sourced through supply chains controlled by the CCP.

When COVID struck, China:
- bought up or seized global supplies of PPE, masks, gloves, ventilator parts
- blocked outbound shipments of medical-grade materials

then sold them back to desperate nations at inflated prices.

When a host depends on the parasite for survival, the host is no longer sovereign.

China didn't need to cut off America's medicine; *the threat of doing so was enough to force silence.*

2. The Solar Panel "Green Trap" — Eco-Dependence by Design

China did not merely dominate the solar panel market. It captured

every link of the chain, from raw materials to finished panels. And how?
- using slave labor in Xinjiang to reduce costs
- subsidizing factories until Western companies collapsed
- flooding markets with cheap panels then raising prices once competitors disappeared

American "green energy" advocates unknowingly built a system where cutting U.S. emissions requires increasing Chinese power.

The parasite grows stronger every time the host believes it is healing itself.

3. Rare Earth Refining — America Sold the Keys to Its Own Future

America once mined and refined rare earth elements—critical for magnets, missiles, drones, electric vehicles, and advanced electronics.

Then China made an offer: "Let us buy your refining plant. We'll handle the dirty work. You can buy from us later."

And American leadership, focused on quarterly profits, agreed.

The result?
- China now controls **over 90%** of global rare-earth processing
- America cannot build advanced weapons without Chinese materials: the host cannot defend itself without the parasite.

The roach walks into the burrow—not because it is forced, but because it has forgotten how to recognize danger.

4. Fentanyl Precursors — Chemical Warfare Without Bullets
Nearly every fentanyl precursor used by Mexican cartels is manufactured in China. This is not accidental.

China:
- exports the chemicals
- trains cartel chemists
- launders the profits
- denies responsibility

Meanwhile, over **70,000 Americans a year** die from synthetic opioids. This is the equivalent of a yearly Vietnam War—but with no soldiers, no bullets, and no headlines.

The parasite doesn't need armies when it can harvest a nation's youth chemically.

5. Intellectual Property Theft on a Civilizational Scale
The CCP has stolen, copied, or reverse-engineered:
- aviation technology
- stealth coatings
- advanced chipset designs
- agricultural genomics
- pharmaceutical formulas
- telecommunications infrastructure
- military drone technology

By some estimates, **up to $600 billion per year** in American innovation flows into China's industrial base. The fungus doesn't need to grow its own genius when it can steal the genius of the host.

6. The Corporate Leash — Wall Street's Will, Not China's

American corporations and financial houses are not victims of China's strategy—they are *partners* in it. BlackRock, Vanguard, MSCI, and others:

- push American pension money into Chinese firms
- reward U.S. companies for offshoring to China
- pressure corporations to comply with Chinese censorship
- lobby the U.S. government *on China's behalf* to keep markets open

This is not infiltration. It is invitation. "Americans are funding their own demise."

The parasite does not need to conquer the host. It only needs the host to seek profit more than survival.

Using the Host's Systems Against Itself

Every system that once belonged to the roach now nourishes the parasite. China has mastered this strategy on an industrial scale.

It is not simply that Beijing spies, steals, infiltrates, and manipulates. It is that America financially fuels its own displacement.

Wall Street giants—BlackRock, Vanguard, State Street—take the retirement funds of American workers and pour billions into Chinese state-backed enterprises built on slave labor, captive ethnic minorities, and wages that approximate economic servitude. The result?

- American pensions look "profitable."
- China's industrial base grows stronger.
- U.S. manufacturers are undercut and shuttered.
- Entire American towns lose their factories.
- Middle-class jobs vanish.

China becomes the world's workshop using American capital. This is not an accidental side effect. It is a feedback loop: ***Americans fund the very machine that destroys their livelihoods.***

This is not incompetence. It is surrender. And no nation survives long when its leaders profit from the parasite as the host collapses beneath them.

Rome fell the same way—a wealthy aristocracy insulated from the consequences of its decisions, and a hollowed middle class unable to sustain the republic.

A nation without a middle class is not a nation. It is a caste system waiting for collapse.

China understood this before we did. And like the wasp, it merely nudges the host into the burrow—and the host walks in willingly, unaware that its own strength is being redirected to incubate someone else's future.

The Pattern in Nature Is the Pattern in Nations

Scripture warned us before science revealed the fungus or wasp:

- *"A little leaven leavens the whole lump."* — Galatians 5:9
- *"Wolves in sheep's clothing."* — Matthew 7:15
- *"False brothers secretly brought in."* — Galatians 2:4
- *"Those who crept in unnoticed."* — Jude 4

The pattern is always the same: infiltration, invasion, use your own strengths against you. Whether in nature or societal structures, that pattern holds: Entry → Hijack → Redirect → Parallel Structure → Weaponization → Replacement.

This is:

- **Marxism's** long march through the institutions
- **Islamism's** formation of cultural enclaves
- **China's** unrestricted war on American sovereignty

They do not need to storm the walls. They only need the host to forget who it is.

Why These Parables Matter for America

We will not forget the ant climbing to its destruction or the roach walking into captivity.

Because now we see the pattern:
- Universities climbing the ideological stalk
- Cities walking into policies that hollow them out
- Churches silencing themselves
- Media echoing narratives crafted elsewhere
- Families losing the ability to recognize danger

Parallel societies flourish not where invaders are strongest, but where the host is weak and hollow.

Missoula is not the fungus.

Dearborn is not the wasp.

But the pattern is real.

And even the sleepiest watchman can understand it now. A civilization does not fall in a single moment. It bleeds out slowly—one concession, one compromise, one captured institution at a time—until it wakes up and finds that its will is no longer its own.

You don't need a prophet to see what's happening. You just need the honesty to admit it. *We're being eaten alive by the very systems we built*—and unless something changes, there won't be enough of the host left to save.

This is what happens when a nation trades vigilance for comfort, conviction for profit, and truth for the approval of men.

If we don't stand now, our children will inherit a country that no longer remembers who we were—or who we were meant to be. But if the children remember, they will not forgive a generation that watched the parasite feed on the host and chose silence.

The Resistance Begins

A hollow host can be restored.
A confused culture can be renewed.
A weakened church can be revived.
...But first we have to look, without flinching, at the rot in our own house.

That's where we're headed next.

11

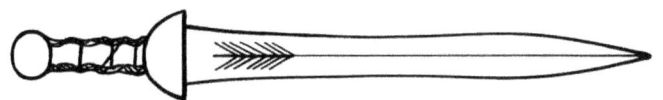

Color Revolution
How Nations Fall — and How the Church Must Stand

Every generation encounters tension and unrest, but only a small number ever face what political theorists now call a *Color Revolution* — a moment when the internal life of a nation becomes the very mechanism of its own undoing.

In a color revolution, the traditional signs of invasion are absent. There are no armies on the beaches, no tanks at the city gates, no foreign generals issuing commands. Instead, a society finds itself slowly unmade from within. The same freedoms that once empowered a people to flourish are strategically weaponized to destabilize them. The same institutions that once protected liberty become instruments of ideological pressure. The same cultural vocabulary that once sustained unity is reshaped to generate perpetual suspicion and moral confusion.

It is no exaggeration to say that America has entered such a moment. And the church — God help us — can no longer avoid naming what is now unfolding in plain sight. This chapter is not a political argument. It is reconnaissance for the faithful. We will explore what a color revolution is, how it operates, why America now fits the pattern, and what role the Christian community must play in a moment that may define the future of the republic.

What a Color Revolution Really Is

A color revolution is not an internet rumor or a partisan accusation. It is a well-established political strategy — one that has reshaped governments in Eastern Europe, Eurasia, and the Middle East. At its core, a color revolution follows a predictable sequence that does not rely on military might. Instead, it relies on mobilized activism, narrative control, ideological coordination, and the systematic erosion of national confidence.

It begins with **weaponized social unrest**. Real grievances — whether economic, racial, or political — are amplified by activists and institutions who see turmoil not as a tragedy to heal, but as an opportunity to steer. Protests evolve into prolonged agitation. Riots are reframed as cries for justice. Unrest becomes a lever to pry open the internal structure of a nation.

The second movement is **narrative control**. Media, universities, entertainment, and digital platforms begin to select and shape information rather than simply report it. They redefine vocabulary, recast history, and determine which voices may be heard. The public no longer receives facts; it receives approved interpretation. Control the narrative, and you control the trajectory of the nation.

The third step is the **delegitimization of existing authority**. Leaders — especially elected leaders — are steadily portrayed as threats to democracy, enemies of progress, or embodiments of oppression. Constitutional structures are condemned as outdated. Law enforcement is framed as inherently unjust. The nation begins to doubt the legitimacy of its own foundations.

Next comes **elite coordination**. Corporate boardrooms, academic departments, government agencies, NGOs, and philanthropic networks begin to move in ideological unison. What appears at first glance to be spontaneous cultural change is more accurately recognized as synchronized institutional pressure. When institutions that once acted independently now speak with one voice, it is not coincidence. It is strategy.

All of this produces **moral confusion** — a condition in which citizens are no longer sure what is true, what is good, what is lawful, or even what is real. A society that cannot define truth cannot defend itself. A society that doubts its own goodness cannot withstand attack. Confusion becomes the soil in which the final phase grows.

The result is **regime replacement**. Once disoriented, the public becomes increasingly willing to accept a new ideological order — one that promises stability, justice, and clarity, but at the cost of freedom, conscience, and religious conviction. In this way, a color revolution does not conquer a nation by force; it conquers by reshaping the nation's moral imagination.

Is America Experiencing a Color Revolution?

Measured by these criteria, America is displaying every hallmark of a society undergoing a color revolution. The signs are not subtle. They are systemic.

In recent years, cities burned as riots were excused as "mostly peaceful protests." Police departments were defunded or dismantled. Statues fell. Neighborhoods were overtaken by autonomous zones. The unrest was justified not as lawlessness, but as moral catharsis — the first unmistakable sign of weaponized upheaval. Consider, theft is termed reparations...when it is just theft.

At the same time, the institutions responsible for public meaning — the media, universities, and digital platforms — ceased to act as neutral arbiters. They began shaping narratives with precision, filtering dissent, redefining language, and elevating one ideological lens above all others. This concentration of narrative control is the second unmistakable marker. The memo goes out and all of a sudden the same phrase is repeated again and again on different networks and different mediums.

Meanwhile, nearly every foundational pillar of American identity came under coordinated assault. The Founders were recast as villains. The Constitution was portrayed as a relic. Law enforcement became inherently suspect. Free markets were equated with injustice. Borders were deemed immoral. Biblical morality was dismissed as bigotry. Christianity — once the moral anchor of the nation — was labeled an obstacle to progress. These are the telltale signs of delegitimization.

Layered on top of all this was the cooperation of elite institutions. Corporations poured millions into activist movements. Willingly or not. Government bureaucracies acted as ideological enforcers. Universities developed pipelines of ideological training. NGOs operated like unelected, unaccountable power centers. The coordination was not accidental. It was structural.

Finally, the moral confusion that now saturates American life is profound. We find ourselves unable to define a man or a woman; unsure of the meaning of family; divided on the nature of justice; uncertain of national boundaries; and hesitant to affirm the basic moral categories that once shaped our common life. A society that cannot define a child, a citizen, or a truth claim is a society prepared — even if unwillingly — for ideological takeover.

All of this reveals a nation undergoing the textbook process of a color revolution.

Why the Three Great Threats Converge Here

The forces now pressing upon America are diverse — Marxism, Islamism, and the Chinese Communist Party — yet they converge on a single shared conviction: **a Christian America stands in their way**.

For Marxists, Christianity is the rival moral order — the one force that insists on objective truth and transcendent morality.

For Islamists, Christianity is the competing religious authority that must be subordinated for the sake of an all-encompassing political theology.

For the CCP, Christianity represents the one feature of human identity that an authoritarian state cannot control: a conscience bound to God rather than to government.

Though these three forces differ in belief, method, and vision, they are united in their opposition to a nation grounded in Scripture, governed by conscience, and shaped by the dignity of being made in the image of God. Their convergence is not coincidence. It is inevitability.

The Scripture Words for This Moment: *Kairos* and *Krisis*
The Bible has language for moments just like this. The first word is ***kairos*** — not merely chronological time, but the appointed moment, the hinge of history when decisions must be made and truth must be revealed. Jesus launched His public ministry with the pronouncement, "The *kairos* is fulfilled" (Mark 1:15). Paul declared that Christ died "at the right *kairos*" (Romans 5:6). A *kairos* is a turning point, a divine intersection where the trajectory of history bends.

But *kairos* is always accompanied by a second word: ***krisis*** — judgment, exposure, revelation. John describes the arrival of Jesus with these piercing words: *"This is the **krisis**: light has come into the world..."* (John 3:19). Christ did not create darkness; He revealed it. His coming exposed the condition of the human heart the way a flawless painting exposes the critic.

In an art museum, two men were standing before an acknowledged master painting. One man began criticizing the brush strokes, the use of lighting, the composition. After his remarks, he walked away. The man who remained admiring the painting, commented, "That man was not judging the painting; the painting was judging him."

In that same way, the coming of Jesus, judged our world merely by his presence.

We are living in a similar moment now. America's turmoil is not merely political. It is a *krisis* — a revealing of our national soul, a moment when the light exposes what has been hidden in shadows. The confusion, hostility, and upheaval are not only signs of cultural breakdown. They are signs of spiritual exposure.

A color revolution cannot gain traction in a morally grounded nation. It requires spiritual weakness, cultural exhaustion, and institutional hollowness. It thrives where people no longer know who they are or what they stand for. In that sense, America's color revolution is as much a spiritual crisis as a political one.

Why the Christian Community Is the Essential Counterforce
If America is experiencing a color revolution, then the only institution capable of resisting it is the one institution the revolution must neutralize to succeed: ***the church of Jesus Christ***.

This is not because the church seeks political dominance or national supremacy. It is because the church alone possesses the moral clarity, the theological vision, and the spiritual authority to speak truth in a moment of deception. A color revolution requires the collapse of objective truth. It requires the absence of transcendent authority. It requires a population willing to be defined by ideology rather than by God.

When the church goes silent, a nation becomes vulnerable. When pulpits trade courage for comfort, the people lose their compass. When believers retreat from public witness, the public square becomes occupied by whatever ideology shouts the loudest.

But history shows something else as well: God's people have always been fashioned for *kairos* moments. The church has stood before Rome, Islam, Communism, fascism, and every manner of revolution. And in every age, when darkness surged, the light did not retreat — it grew brighter.

America's shaking is not the end. It is the summons. This is the moment when the church must recover its voice, rediscover its resolve, and reclaim its mission. Pastors must speak plainly. Believers must stand boldly. Churches must once again become anchors of truth, not shelters of retreat.

Critical Mass
We are approaching a critical mass in America. Violence is rising, order is eroding, and trust in institutions is collapsing. Paul makes it clear in Romans 13 that the state bears real responsibility — not symbolic responsibility — to protect its citizens and to punish those who commit evil. That mandate applies to every citizen, of every origin, who lives under our laws. When people break those laws, justice is not optional. It is required.

This is where the church must recover its spine. Soft Christianity wants only the God of mercy and forgets the God of justice. It preaches love but ignores holiness. It speaks of compassion but avoids accountability. The God of Scripture is not divided. His attributes are not in tension. His mercy means nothing without His righteousness, and His love means nothing without His truth.

If the church is to stand in this moment, it must again embrace the whole counsel of God. Otherwise, we become, to borrow a biblical image, wheat crushed under the millstone of the very ideologies we warn against. The moment calls for resolve, courage, and justice without apology — doing everything faith allows and everything justice demands.

This Is the Inflection Point

We stand now at a *kairos* — a God-ordained moment when nations either repent or fall. If the church wakes, America may yet endure. If the church sleeps, America will inevitably pass under a new regime.

We are the last generation that will live free if we do nothing — and we are the first generation that will live faithfully if we stand.

Christians do not resist with violence. We resist with truth, with courage, with repentance, and with the public proclamation of the Gospel.

But resist we must. If we remain silent, the color will drain from the American flag until nothing remains but the gray of subjugation.

This is the inflection point.

This is the battlefield.

This is the trumpet call.

And having done all — by the grace of God — **we will stand**.

12

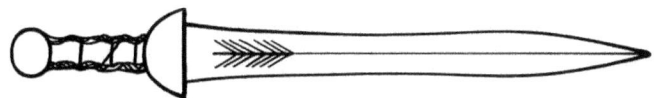

Why We Are Weak
The Rot That Grew While We Slept
The Enemies Within

The parasites are real. But they flourish most where the host is already weakened. America has always faced external enemies — empires, ideologies, movements that sought to weaken or replace the constitutional order. But the enemies within have always been the most dangerous. A nation can withstand siege from the outside. It cannot survive rot from the inside.

And that is precisely where we now stand.

For years we focused on Marxists in our universities, Islamists building parallel societies, and China's unrestricted warfare threading through our economy. But while those forces grew bold, another threat matured quietly in the shadows of our own institutions.

- Corrupt politicians, greedy financiers, and unchecked tech oligarchs did not storm the gates.
  They *became* the gatekeepers.
- They did not march into Washington as conquerors.
  They turned Washington into their marketplace.
- They did not overthrow the nation

They slowly bought pieces of it — policy by policy, regulation by regulation, platform by platform.

These are the enemies without uniforms. The enemies with suits instead of swords. The enemies who understood the simplest law in all of political life: If the people sleep, someone else will write the rules.

While Americans raised families and built businesses, these internal actors quietly rewired the system:

- **Corrupt officials** traded power for influence, and influence for cash.
- **Financial elites** turned risk into profit but losses into bailouts.
- **Tech oligarchs** built platforms larger than nations, with more data than governments, and with less accountability than either.

Together they formed something America had never seen before: a ruling class with no loyalty to the people and no fear of the consequences. If you map the richest counties in America, the truth screams off the page. Five of the top ten sit in the shadow of Washington, D.C.—the permanent home of lobbyists, bureaucrats, contractors, and the political class.

"The hogs don't wander far from the trough."

These counties don't produce goods. They don't innovate. They don't manufacture. They *extract*—from the taxpayer, from federal budgets, from regulatory capture, from the machinery of influence.

The other cluster tells the rest of the story.

Four of the remaining top ten counties surround Silicon Valley—a region that now functions as America's unregulated Ministry of Information.

- Platforms larger than nations.

- Data repositories deeper than intelligence agencies.
- Algorithms capable of shaping elections, markets, public opinion, and the moral intuitions of an entire generation.

What does the map show?

Two power centers—***D.C. and Silicon Valley***—now hold more wealth, more influence, and more control over American life than any democratic framework ever envisioned.

- Not a single farm county.
- Not a manufacturing region.
- Not an energy hub.
- Not a community that actually produces the goods that keep the nation alive.

This is the new American aristocracy: bureaucratic power in the east, technological power in the west, and ordinary Americans squeezed between them.

It is no accident that the counties closest to the federal purse and the counties closest to the digital surveillance infrastructure are the wealthiest in the nation.

The map is not whispering. It is shouting. And what it shouts is simple: **Our richest regions are those that govern us—not those that sustain us.**

What foreign enemies attempted in decades, internal elites accomplished in years—not through invasion—through erosion. And the miracle is not that America is falling now. The miracle is that it stood this long with such rot in the beams.

Because here is the truth polite society refuses to say out loud: *A nation can survive Marxists in the classroom, Islamists in the enclave, and China in the supply chain — but it cannot survive betrayal from its own leaders.*

When the guardians become grifters, when institutions become instruments, when laws become tools for the powerful instead of protections for the powerless, a nation does not simply weaken. It is devoured from within.

The enemies from without exploit the cracks. The enemies from within create them. And if we do not confront this internal rot — courageously, soberly, relentlessly — then all the warnings about Marxism, Islamism, and China will amount to little more than commentary on why the collapse came sooner than it should have.

The truth is sobering, but necessary: *America will not fall because its enemies were too strong. America will fall because its people waited too long to confront those who devoured it from within.*

Here we stand — not too late, not defeated, not without options.
The <u>first step</u> toward restoration is the courage to name the rot.
The <u>second</u> is to refuse to tolerate it.
The <u>third</u> is to rebuild what we once allowed to decay.

Nothing New Under the Sun

What we face is not new. The pattern is older than America, older than empires, older than any ideology. Whenever a people grow complacent, whenever their elites grow corrupt, whenever the walls of moral order crumble from the inside—God leaves us a witness in Scripture to show us what comes next, and what must be done. And the clearest of those witnesses is Nehemiah.

Nehemiah: The Enemies Without—and the Enemies Within

The story of Nehemiah is not merely ancient history. It is a mirror. Hold it up, and you will see America staring back.

Jerusalem was in ruins—not because the walls had fallen, but because the people had. The gates were burned. The economy was broken. The culture was humiliated. The temple stood, but the nation had lost its center.

And into this moment God raised a man—not a priest, not a prophet, not a king, but a public servant with a burden strong enough to move empires. But the moment Nehemiah set his hand to rebuilding, two kinds of enemies emerged—just as they always do in times of national vulnerability.

1. The Enemies from Without: Open Opposition

Nehemiah faced external enemies who openly sought to undermine the rebuilding:
- Sanballat the Horonite
- Tobiah the Ammonite
- Geshem the Arab

These men were power brokers—regional actors with political sway. They had every interest in keeping Jerusalem weak, divided, impoverished, and defenseless.

And their tactics mirror the adversaries America faces today:
- Ridicule to break morale
- Rumors to sow confusion
- Psychological warfare to instill fear
- Political pressure to halt progress
- Threats of violence to force compliance

Nehemiah never romanticized their intentions. He never pretended they were "misunderstood neighbors." He recognized them as hostile actors seeking to exploit a weakened people.

America has its Sanballats and Geshems today—Marxists, Islamists, and the architects of China's unrestricted warfare. And like Nehemiah, we fool ourselves if we minimize what they openly declare.

But Nehemiah understood something deeper: A nation can survive enemies at the gate. It cannot survive those in the house.

Which leads to the second—and more dangerous—category.

2. The Enemies Within: Compromise in the Camp

Nehemiah's greatest obstacles didn't come from outside Jerusalem. They came from within.

A. The Nobles Who Refused to Work (Nehemiah 3:5)

"The nobles would not put their shoulders to the work."
These were the elites—comfortable, privileged, insulated. They benefited from the system as it was and saw no reason to change.

Sound familiar?

From Washington's suburbs to Silicon Valley, America's highest incomes cluster around political power and technological power—the new ruling class. They prosper whether the nation succeeds or fails.

So did the nobles of Jerusalem.

B. Jewish Leaders Making Private Deals with the Enemy (Nehemiah 6:17–19)

This is the shocker in the narrative. While Nehemiah fought Sanballat and Tobiah, the nobles of Judah were secretly aligned with them.
- They exchanged letters.
- They shared intelligence.
- They protected Tobiah's influence.
- They undermined Nehemiah's work behind his back.

Nehemiah was trying to rebuild the wall. They were trying to rebuild their alliances.

This is *precisely* what America faces today with its internal elites:
- Lobbyists who circle Washington like satellites around a planet
- Politicians who trade access for cash
- Financiers who privatize profits and socialize losses
- Tech oligarchs who know more about our people than our government does
- Corporate giants who exploit cheap labor abroad while gutting the American middle class
- Media empires who craft narratives that serve ideology rather than truth

Just as in Nehemiah's day, the internal corruption doesn't merely weaken resistance—it empowers the enemies outside the walls.

C. Usury and Exploitation of the Poor (Nehemiah 5)
Before Nehemiah ever picks up a sword or trowel, he confronts a domestic crisis: The wealthy were taking the homes, fields, and children of the poor as collateral.

In other words: Jerusalem's internal economy was destroying its own people.

Nehemiah burns with righteous anger: *"You are exacting usury, each from his brother!"* — Nehemiah 5:7

Does it sound familiar?
- 2008: Wall Street gambles, Main Street pays.
- COVID: Big box stores grow fat, small businesses die.
- Pharma: Record profits while opioid-ravaged communities bury their young.

- Tech: Billionaires track us with devices we willingly carry—"a tracking device that happens to make calls."
- DC: Five of America's richest counties living off taxpayer-funded power.

Nehemiah saw the same pattern: A corrupt elite enriching themselves at the expense of the people they were supposed to serve.

3. The Leadership Model America Forgot

Nehemiah shows what righteous leadership looks like in a nation under pressure:
1. He prayed.
2. He planned.
3. He built.
4. He confronted corruption.
5. He exposed compromise.
6. He armed the people.
7. He finished the work.

He did not run. He did not retreat. He did not rationalize. He did not spiritualize away his responsibility. *And when the internal enemies tried to pull him into meaningless meetings with the external enemies, he gave the line every American leader should memorize: "I am doing a great work and I cannot come down.*
— Nehemiah 6:3

A Wall-Builder in Our Time

My friend Robert Washington understood Nehemiah because he lived Nehemiah.

Robert was a bi-vocational pastor—a preacher of the Word and a mason by trade. At six-foot-four and nearly three hundred pounds, he stood as solid as the brick and stone walls he built with his own hands. He knew what it meant to labor with weight, patience, and purpose. Walls are not raised by talk. They are built course by course, stone by stone, with steady, strong hands.

He served in the African-American community and often faced opposition because he refused to stay in prescribed lanes. He crossed racial lines without apology, serving alongside white, Hispanic, Chinese, and Korean congregations in a shared association of churches. That kind of work invites resistance—sometimes from the outside, sometimes from within. Robert understood both.

He had a rare gift of discernment. When tensions rose and motives blurred, he could see through posturing and name what was really at work. He did not inflame conflict; he steadied it. He offered quiet counsel when others rushed to noise. He labored to bridge chasms of race, suspicion, and old wounds—not with slogans, but with faithfulness.

As a mason, Robert carried his skills to mission fields, leaving his mark in stone in places where churches were being built—places where the gospel would be preached, believers discipled, and communities gathered in fellowship. He knew that walls matter when they protect what is good and sacred. He also knew that walls must be built while others stand guard.

That is why he loved Nehemiah.

Nehemiah was a wall-builder, too. And when enemies tried to distract him—when they sought to pull him down from the work with false meetings and manufactured urgency—Nehemiah answered with words Robert quoted often and lived daily: *"I am doing a great work, and I cannot come down."* — Nehemiah 6:3

Robert did not come down. Not from the work. Not from the calling. Not from the responsibility God had placed in his hands. He built, he guarded, he discerned, and he finished what he was given to do.

America has forgotten this kind of leadership. But the pattern remains—for those with eyes to see it.

Nehemiah's leadership did not end with ancient walls; it still appears wherever men and women refuse distraction, face opposition with clarity, and finish the work God sets before them.

4. The Lesson for America

The parallels are unmistakable:
- Enemies at the gate
- Enemies in the bureaucracy
- Enemies in the economy
- Enemies in the cultural institutions
- Enemies in the halls of power

And in the midst of all of it—a people unsure of their identity, their calling, or their mission.

Nehemiah rebuilt a wall in 52 days because he did what America has forgotten to do:
- Name the enemies
- Expose the corruption
- Rally the righteous
- Arm the vulnerable
- Stand against intimidation
- Restore moral order
- Rebuild what was broken
- Unite God's people around truth

If America remembers Nehemiah, there is hope. If it forgets him, it will suffer the fate of every nation that let internal corruption finish the work that external enemies began.

13

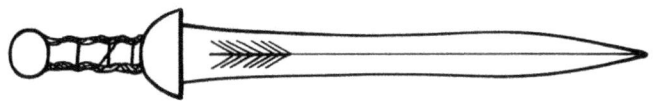

The Great Unraveling
How America Lost Its Immune System

Before a society collapses outwardly, it collapses inwardly.
Before enemies infiltrate its borders, lies infiltrate its classrooms.
Before a nation loses its freedoms, it loses its memory.

Bill Lincoln said it plainly at Sykes Diner: **"Sometimes I hate the truth."** But he said it with a grin—because truth is what sets us free, and truth is what brought us to this chapter.

Our vulnerability did not appear overnight. It was cultivated—classroom by classroom, pulpit by pulpit, policy by policy—until we created a generation unable to discern truth, defend it, or even recognize when it was under attack.

If you want to understand—
why Missoula is vulnerable…
why Dearborn happened…
why Marxism reigns in universities…
why Islamist enclaves grow bold…

why China walks through our institutions like an open door...

Then, we must understand the slow demolition of American education and the parallel retreat of the American church.

This is the story of how the host lost its immune system.

1. When a Nation Forgets Its Foundations

America's strength was never primarily in its wealth, weapons, or political machinery. Its strength was in its **worldview**—a people shaped, however imperfectly, by the moral grammar of Scripture.

Even non-believers benefited from it. Even secular institutions relied upon it.

But when spiritual foundations erode, everything built upon them crumbles.

> **"If the foundations are destroyed, what can the righteous do?" — Psalm 11:3**

For the first 150 years of American life, schools reinforced these foundations:

- prayer
- the Ten Commandments
- biblical literacy
- moral reasoning
- civic virtue

Not indoctrination—**formation**. But beginning in the 1960s, a cultural revolution began—not with guns, but with court decisions, unions, curriculum committees, publishing houses, and ideological infiltration.

Brick by brick, the foundations were removed:
- **1962 — School prayer removed**
- **1963 — Scripture reading removed**
- **1980 — The Ten Commandments banned from classroom walls**

The Supreme Court did not merely remove religious practices. It removed memory—memory of where moral authority comes from.

And the great unraveling began.

2. A Curriculum Rewritten to Produce Amnesia
When truth is removed, ideology rushes in to fill the vacuum. Bill Lincoln lived through it as an educator. He watched the textbooks shift, the language morph, the narratives mutate.

Three massive distortions followed:

A. History Rewritten
America—once understood as a flawed but extraordinary experiment in liberty—was recast as an irredeemably oppressive project. The *1619 Project*, discredited by scholars across the political spectrum, was injected into classrooms as gospel truth. Students stopped learning *what* happened, and were taught *how to interpret it* before they ever read it.

B. Science Politicized
Biology bowed to gender ideology.
Data bowed to climate ideology.
Speech bowed to DEI ideology.
Truth became whatever the ideology needed.

C. Language Weaponized
Critical Race Theory divided students into permanent castes—oppressor and oppressed.

"Equity" replaced equality.

"Safety" meant ideological conformity.

"Tolerance" became mandatory approval.

Reshape language, and you reshape thought. Reshape thought, and you reshape culture.

This is not education. It is indoctrination. It is the Gramscian playbook—executed inside the classroom walls.

3. A Teaching Force Captured by Ideological Unions
Bill is right: **"The teachers' unions have too much power."**

The NEA and AFT—the two largest teachers' unions—are no longer educational bodies. They are ideological engines. They:

- fought to keep schools closed during the Covid outbreak
- pushed DEI bureaucracies
- wrote curriculum guidelines
- funded political campaigns
- opposed parental oversight
- framed dissent as "extremism"

And they shield underperforming teachers from accountability—guaranteeing that ideology replaces excellence.

A nation cannot remain strong when its children are shaped by a system hostile to its values.

4. The Dumbing Down of a People
Why are Americans vulnerable to Marxism, Islamism, authoritarianism, propaganda, emotional manipulation, and identity politics?

Because we have produced a people who cannot think biblically, historically, or logically. This is not an insult. It is a diagnosis. Look at what has been lost—

A. Critical Thinking Gone
Students aren't taught to reason—only to repeat.

B. Biblical Literacy Gone
Hebrews 5:12–14 describes this generation:
"Infants in need of milk... unskilled in the word."

C. Doctrinal Clarity Gone
1 Corinthians 3:1–3 calls it what it is: **spiritual infancy.**

D. Moral Confidence Gone
Students are trained so that they cannot judge:
- culture
- behavior
- ideas
- ideology
- religion

A nation that cannot judge evil cannot defend against it.

And this brings us to the hinge.
This is where education's collapse meets the church's retreat.

5. Where the Schools Fell, the Church Slept
The story of America's unraveling does not begin in courtrooms or legislatures. It begins in classrooms. But it does not end there.

When the schools abandoned truth, the church should have surged forward with clarity.
It didn't.

When prayer and Scripture were stripped from public education, the church should have strengthened its own teaching—doubling down on doctrine, worldview, and moral formation.
It didn't.

When new ideologies poured into the vacuum—Marxist frameworks, racialized theories, gender dogma—the church should have trained its people to recognize falsehood by the light of Scripture.
It didn't.

The collapse in the schools and the confusion in the pulpits were not two unrelated failures. They were two halves of the same story. Two doors left unguarded. Two foundations left unattended. Two watchtowers without watchmen.

The schools removed the knowledge of God.
The church stopped proclaiming the authority of God.

Together, they created a generation that could not remember truth—and a generation that could not recognize a lie. It was the perfect storm. In the vacuum left by educational amnesia, the church might have stepped forward as the nation's last teacher of moral clarity, biblical literacy, and disciplined thinking.

But instead, many churches softened their message just as the culture hardened its rebellion.

While classrooms taught children that truth is relative, the church preached sermons that made truth optional. While schools redefined human identity, pastors avoided the very passages of Scripture that would have corrected the confusion. While educators trained students in the categories of grievance and power, pulpits retreated into messages of comfort and self-help.

The result? A population formed by secular ideology—and a

church unprepared to confront it.

Schools produce the mind of a nation. Churches shape the conscience of a nation.

When both falter, a people lose not only what they should know, but who they should be.

And now the enemies of freedom—Marxist, Islamist, and global authoritarianism—walk through both doors:
- through the schools that no longer teach discernment,
- and through the churches that no longer practice it.

The great tragedy of our age is not merely that the schools forgot the truth, but that the church forgot its voice. When the schools fell, the church slept.

And the slow collapse of a civilization gained speed.

6. Why Pastors and Churches Failed to Engage the Enemies

Here is the distilled truth:

The enemies of our age did not defeat the church.

The church retreated before the battle began.

A. Eschatology Without Mission

Too many believers were told:

"We're going home soon,"

"It's all going to burn,"

"Don't worry about fixing the world."

So they waited for extraction instead of engaging in mission.

But ambassadors do not hide in the embassy. They engage the kingdom to which they are sent.

B. Withdrawal from the World — Confusing Holiness with Isolation

Jesus prayed:

"They are not of the world" **(identity)**

"I do not ask that You take them out of the world" **(assignment)**
— John 17:14–18

But Christians created parallel subcultures—Christian schools, music, athletics, bookstores—and abandoned civic influence entirely. Salt stayed in the shaker. Light stayed under the basket. And darkness filled the room.

Now public institutions and activities are so corrupted, Christian parents are being forced to keep children separate to maintain their mental and spiritual health...and to keep their bodies intact.

C. Misreading *"Render Unto Caesar"*

When Jesus made the statement to the Pharisees and Herodians to *"Render unto Caesar the things that are Caesar's and unto God the things that are God's"*, He was not commanding political retreat. He was affirming *dual realms* and *dual accountability*. The citizen has responsibilities to both the state and to God.

While believers have been *"translated into the Kingdom of His dear son"* (Col. 1:3), we have not been taken out of the world. We remain in the world as salt and light to preserve and to illuminate as God's witnesses in the world. And in this world we have a stewardship to participate in the political governance (Rms. 13).

When Christians leave governance to the ungodly, the ungodly govern the Christians.

D. The Myth of the Neutral Public Square

Christians assumed institutions were neutral. They were not. And they never are.

Those who shape the schools shape the nation.

Those who shape the language shape the future.

Those who shape the narrative shape the public mind.

While Christians withdrew, the enemies of truth advanced.

E. Misdiagnosing the Mission — Forgetting the Gospel of the Kingdom

Evangelicals excelled at evangelism, prayer, mission, church attendance—but forgot that Jesus preached the *gospel of the Kingdom* (Matthew 4:23). A public, cultural, ethical, transformational Kingdom. And where the church retreated from culture, culture filled the vacancy with another kingdom.

The Result: A Retreating Church in an Advancing Age of Darkness

Christians withdrew.
Enemies advanced.
Pastors stayed silent.
Wolves filled the silence.

The church that should have been salt became a spectator.
The church that should have been light became invisible.
The church that should have stood in the gate stood on the sidelines.

And now, even those who once said, "We shouldn't get involved," whisper, "We may have waited too long."

The Turning Point

When the church forgets its calling, the world forgets its God.
When the world forgets its God, its enemies claim their moment.
But here is the hope:
A single courageous pastor is worth a hundred silent ones.
A single church can reshape a county.
A movement of awakened believers can turn a nation.

Education created the vacuum. The church left it empty. Now comes the moment to reverse both the church's and the world's failures.

The Resistance Begins

A hollow host can be restored.

A confused culture can be renewed.

A weakened church can be revived.

But only by returning to the center— to truth, Scripture, identity, and Christ.

"Having done all, to stand firm." — **Ephesians 6:13**

14

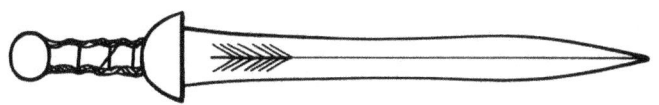

The Men of Issachar
Discernment, Stewardship, and the Duty of a Generation

"And of the sons of Issachar, men who understood the times, with knowledge of what Israel should do, their chiefs were two hundred; and all their kinsmen were at their command."
— 1 Chronicles 12:32

Every generation is tested—but not every generation recognizes its test.

> Some misread the moment and sleep.
> Others see the signs but lack the courage to act.
> Only a few discern the hour clearly and understand what faithfulness requires.

Scripture remembers those few. The sons of Issachar did not win Israel's battles by strength of arms alone. Their gift was discernment. They understood the times. They recognized where history stood, what forces were moving, and what obedience required now, not in some idealized past or deferred future. Their wisdom stabilized a nation at a moment of transition, when confusion could have shattered unity and delay could have proved fatal.

That same burden rests upon us.

This book has traced the long war—how ideas prepared the

ground for institutions to fall; how infiltration proved more effective than invasion; how Marxism hollowed the mind, Islamism tested the will, and authoritarian regimes like Communist China learned to exploit a weakened republic. We have named enemies without and enemies within. We have followed the slow rot that weakened the beams while the house still looked sound.

Now comes the necessary question: Do we understand the times? Because discernment without action is merely observation. And observation without obedience is another form of retreat.

Discernment Is a Moral Responsibility

The sons of Issachar were not applauded because they were insightful commentators. They were honored because their understanding moved the nation. Their discernment carried obligation. Once times were understood, indecision was no longer an option.

That is where many modern Christians stumble:

- We assess.
- We analyze.
- We lament.
- We share articles.
- We shake our heads.

But Scripture never treats insight as an endpoint. Knowledge that does not lead to obedience becomes a liability.

Jesus rebuked those who could read the skies but not the signs of the times (Matthew 16:3). To see clearly and still refuse to act is not humility—it is negligence. It leaves the gate open.

We are no longer living in an age where the threat is ambiguous. The cultural, moral, and spiritual battlelines are visible. The systems shaping our children, our language, our economy, and our public life are openly hostile to biblical truth. Neutrality is no longer a tenable position.

The sons of Issachar *knew what Israel should do*. That phrase matters.

Not merely what Israel could do.

Not merely what Israel discussed doing.

But what Israel should do.

Citizenship Is Stewardship in a Republic

Here we must confront a misunderstanding that has paralyzed much of the church.

Some believers assume that civic disengagement is a form of spiritual purity—as though holiness requires withdrawal from responsibility. But Scripture does not support that view. In fact, it contradicts it.

Romans 13:1–7 teaches that governing authority exists by God's design, not as an accident of history. Authority is accountable to God, and those who live under that authority bear responsibility for how it is ordered.

- In a monarchy, responsibility concentrates in a king.
- In a tyranny, power consolidates in a few.
- But in a republic, authority is distributed among the people.

That reality carries profound moral weight. Romans 13 does not call Christians to passivity; it calls them to submission to the governing order God has established. In a republic, that order does not rest in a throne or a ruling caste—it rests in the people themselves. Authority flows upward from the citizen, not downward from a crown. To submit to governing authority in such a system necessarily involves participation in it. We are the government.

When Christians withdraw from civic responsibility under the banner of spiritual purity, they do not honor Romans 13—they hollow it out. Submission, in this context, is not silence. It is stewardship. It is the faithful exercise of the responsibility God has entrusted to citizens to shape law, restrain evil, and promote the common good. Refusing that responsibility does not keep one unstained; it leaves the field to those who do not share Christian convictions.

This is not a call to political idolatry or partisan obsession. It is a call to obedience rightly understood. The New Testament never envisions a people who pray for rulers while refusing to act as citizens when the structure of government demands their voice. In a republic, disengagement is not neutrality—it is abdication. When the righteous retreat, authority does not disappear; it is simply seized by others.

To participate, then, is not to compromise the gospel. It is to preserve the conditions under which the gospel may be freely preached, believed, and lived. Citizenship, rightly exercised, becomes an act of love—love for neighbor, love for future generations, and love for the truth that cannot flourish where responsibility has been surrendered.

That changes everything.

In a republic, citizenship is stewardship. To withdraw from that stewardship is not holiness—it is abdication. When Christians refuse to participate, they do not create a neutral space; they simply hand influence to those who do not share their convictions. When the righteous retreat, the unrighteous govern unchecked.

This is not a call to partisan frenzy. It is a call to fidelity.

Voting, civic participation, public witness, engagement in schools and communities—these are not distractions from discipleship. They are expressions of it. Christians are stewards not only of the gospel they proclaim, but of the social order in which that gospel is lived.

To bury that stewardship in the ground is not faithfulness. Christ gave a name for that.

The Wall Will Not Rebuild Itself

Nehemiah did not wait for perfect conditions. He recognized that delay favors the enemy. He rebuilt the wall under threat, under ridicule, under internal sabotage. He prayed—and then he planned. He trusted God—and then he armed the people.

Walls do not rebuild themselves.
Institutions do not self-correct.
Cultures do not drift toward truth.

They are rebuilt by people who understand the times and refuse to surrender responsibility.

America's breach is not merely political. It is moral and spiritual. And no court ruling, election cycle, or charismatic leader can substitute for a formed people willing to stand in the gate.

Homes must be reclaimed.
Churches must recover their voice.
Schools must be confronted.
Communities must be engaged.
The public square must no longer be surrendered by default.

This is not alarmism. It is reality. A wall half-rebuilt invites disaster. A people half-awake do not withstand a determined enemy.

This Is a Generational Trust

Not every generation is asked to preserve what it inherited. Some are asked to rebuild what was neglected. That is a heavier calling—but not an unprecedented one.

The sons of Issachar did not lament the complexity of their moment. They rose to it.

So must we. We are not responsible for the decline we inherited. But we are responsible for what we do with the hour we've been given. Silence now is not humility—it is consent. Withdrawal is not prudence—it is surrender.

The war did not begin with us. It will not end with us. But faithfulness demands that we hold the line in our time.

Where This Volume Ends—and the Next Must Begin

This first volume has named the conflict, traced the decay, and exposed the fault lines. Awareness is necessary—but it is not sufficient. Diagnosis without discipline guarantees defeat.

Understanding the times must give way to obedience within them. That is why the work cannot end here. What remains is formation:

- Training.
- Discipline.
- Life in the Spirit.
- A people forged to stand—not merely to see.

That work begins next.

But for now, the charge is clear:
>Understand the times.
>Know what must be done.
>And refuse to surrender the future by silence.

The wall is not finished.
The watch has been handed to us.
And history will record whether this generation understood its hour.

>*"Having done all… to stand firm."*
>— **Ephesians 6:13**

Epilogue

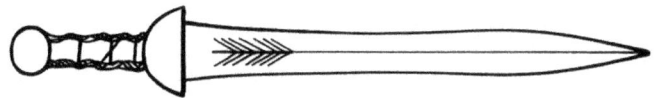

The Watchman's Burden

Nations do not drift into tyranny. They are escorted there by inattentive citizens, silent churches, and leaders who mistake comfort for blessing. But every generation also has its watchmen—those who climb the wall, scan the horizon, and refuse to lie about what they see.

You, reader, have now seen the field.

You have traced the long march of ideas that hollowed out a nation from the inside.

You have watched Marxism exchange textbooks for power.

You have seen Islamism build enclaves within our borders.

You have observed China's patient, strategic encroachment upon every sector of American life.

And you have stared directly at the truth most fear to name: a Republic falls not when its enemies grow strong, but when its people grow weak.

This volume has been about sight—about naming the threats, understanding the siege, and recovering what earlier generations once knew instinctively. But vision alone never saved a nation.

The watchman's task is not merely to observe, but to warn. And the citizen's task is not merely to understand, but to act.

America stands at such a threshold. Not of despair—but of decision.

The next years will determine whether the Republic remains

free or becomes another cautionary tale in the long history of fallen nations. This moment demands clarity, courage, and above all, conviction. It demands men and women who understand the times—and who refuse to surrender their stewardship under the pressure of fear, fatigue, or false comfort.

But understanding the battle is only the beginning. A nation cannot be saved by strategy alone. It must be sustained by character, discipline, and the moral strength of its people.

The walls are rebuilt not by outrage, but by formation. That is why a companion volume exists.

Called to Stand turns from the enemies without to the formation within. From the siege to the soul. From naming the threats to shaping the warriors. From surveying the battlefield to learning how to fight.

If this volume has awakened you, the next will equip you. If this volume has revealed the breach, the next will help you rebuild it. If this volume has clarified the hour, the next will prepare your hands for the work.

We cannot choose the age in which we live. But we can choose the posture in which we stand.

May you take up your place on the battleline—not in fear, but in faith; not in anger, but in allegiance; and not as a spectator, but as a citizen of a Republic worth defending and a Kingdom that cannot be shaken.

The trumpet is sounding.
The warriors are few.
Take your post.

Group Study Guide Available

A free, downloadable Group Study Guide is available at **PGSPublishing.com**. The guide provides a structured, discussion-based formation process for use in churches, men's and women's groups, and civic study groups.

Get the companion volume—

Called to Stand
A Field Manual for the Christian Warrior

If *The Battle for the Republic* names the enemies at the gates, **Called to Stand** equips the warriors within the walls.

In a world where truth is contested, conscience is pressured, and the Church is tempted toward retreat, this companion volume turns from diagnosis to formation. Drawing from Scripture, history, and decades of pastoral leadership, **Called to Stand** lays out the disciplines, doctrines, and spiritual practices needed to build immovable Christians in a collapsing age.

This is not a book of slogans. It is a manual—sharp, grounded, and deeply practical.

Inside these pages, you will explore:

- Life in the Spirit as the engine of endurance
- The disciplined habits that forge spiritual strength
- The armor of God applied to modern battlegrounds
- The restoration of courage in the church and character in the believer
- The call to take your post in the public square with wisdom and conviction

If Volume 1 revealed the breach, Volume 2 teaches you how to rebuild it.

If Volume 1 awakened you, Volume 2 will train your hands for the work.

Whether read on its own or as the essential continuation of *The Battle for the Republic,* **Called to Stand** prepares ordinary believers for extraordinary times—forming a people who can stand firm, speak truth, and carry light into whatever darkness comes next.

Stand your post.
Strengthen your heart.
The battle requires both courage and formation.

Available at Amazon, Barnes & Noble, and retailers across the nation.

Other books by Charles Garner

Beyond Expectations
The Kingdom No One Expected

What kind of Kingdom begins with a cross?
Jesus came preaching the Kingdom of God—but not the one anyone expected.

Beyond Expectations: The Kingdom No One Expected invites you into 55 vivid vignettes—each a devotional window into the life of Jesus and the surprising nature of His reign. From the wedding at Cana to the cry from the cross, these reflections trace the arc of a Kingdom not built on conquest, but on compassion; not rooted in might, but in mercy.

Blending pastoral warmth, poetic insight, and biblical depth, this is **devotional theology**—Scripture brought to life in ways both reverent and real.

Whether read alone or used a guide for Bible study groups, *Beyond Expectations* will draw you deeper into the story of the King who came to save...not the way we imagined—but just as God had planned.

**Step into the Kingdom.
Let it turn your expectations upside down.**

Available at Amazon, Barnes & Noble, and retailers across the nation.

Get the companion to *Beyond Expectations*...

Profiles from Paul
A Life Poured Out for the Kingdom

What Jesus began, Paul explained and extended—through a Spirit-empowered life of mission, message, and ministry. *Profiles from Paul* explores the story of the early church through the eyes of the man who gave structure to the gospel and insight to the Kingdom.

A devotional theology rooted in Acts and the Epistles.

In 75 short, reflective vignettes, the Apostle Paul's life is traced from conversion to calling, from mission to imprisonment. Each vignette includes biblical narrative, historical insight, original poetry, and questions for personal or group reflection.

Written for everyday Christians, this book brings Paul's letters and legacy into focus with warmth, clarity, and conviction. Ideal for personal devotion, small group study, or leadership training, this resource invites readers to walk the path of faith with Paul as their guide.

Available at Amazon, Barnes & Noble, and retailers across the nation.

www.ingramcontent.com/pod-product-compliance
Lightning Source LLC
Chambersburg PA
CBHW060947050426
42337CB00052B/1634